DEATH TO F.R.O.G.S.

BooX AI

DEATH TO F.R.O.G.S.

THE ART OF LIVING

MRJAMES LIFECOACH

CONTENTS

PREFACE

It is not within the author's authority nor his intention to speak neither for nor against the doctrines, principles, concepts, or tenets of any Church. Therefore, as the author discusses his personal beliefs and real-life experiences, the comments by the author and the entirety of the information are to be regarded as his interpretation of the material presented. The author, therefore, assumes all responsibility for its content.

ACKNOWLEDGMENTS

The author takes this opportunity to express sincere thanks to God and gratitude for the enlightenment received from his journey through addiction, jails, rehabs, grief, pain, disappointments, relapse, abstinence, the rooms of recovery, and the recovery process. He is equally thankful for the many prayers offered on his behalf by his wife, Angelia; their daughter, Darnaisha; two sons, Devin and Darrell Jr.; and three granddaughters, Trinity, Mariah, and Morgan.

In the peak of compulsive, obsessive, and destructive addictive behavior, just as everyone was feeling hopeless and helpless, their oldest son, Darrell Jr., said, "Mom, I just believe Dad will beat this thing." Several years later, now finding himself clean, serene, and sober, the author was unable to provide any *real help* to Darrell Jr., who was now at the onset of his own personal struggle of depression and denial. The author will eternally remember the words of encouragement and faith he had heard spoken by this same son years earlier.

Consequently, the suicide death of Darrell Jr., who at the time was silently struggling with depression and denial, is what has motivated the author to share his real-life experiences. This volume is the sharing of personal tragedy as a way to help others and to gain a sense of meaning and purpose for that devastating chapter and period in their family's life.

The author's gratitude to other relatives, friends, fellow

church members, and other associates for their many prayers and their fasting on his behalf is immeasurable. Particular appreciation is acknowledged to all those who were able to separate the destructive addictive conduct and actions from the inner person behind the negative, destructive addictive behavior.

"Death To F.R.O.G.S." is dedicated to you all and in special memory of his dear friend: George Vernon Peterson.

ABOUT THE AUTHOR

Darrell "MrJames" Campbell has been studying the Word of God since age twelve when he first considered the question: "Where did I come from? Why am I here, and where do I go after this life? Where did God come from? Who decided the color of blue would be called blue instead of red, brown, black, or purple; why not call it orange?"

MrJames has continually studied the Word of God, the *Bible*, Scriptures, the *Book of Mormon, Pearl of Great Price, Doctrine and Covenants*, and other inspired sacred writings by Prophets, Apostles, and teachers. His God-given love, devotion, and inclination for spiritual study have guided him in meditating, pondering, reflecting, fasting, and praying for spiritual insight and understanding.

Hundreds of hours of dedicated study have spiritually enlightened his mind with personal understanding, knowledge, and wisdom in *the art of living* according to life's terms and living life on God's terms. Therefore, the practical application of biblical principles has given him *real-life* experience and prepared him to present a unique perspective on the art of living and the recovery process.

Finding himself separated from God, feeling all alone, unable to see himself as a child of God, struggling with substance abuse and destructive addictive behaviors, his thoughts turned back to heaven. MrJames began to reflect upon his mother's favorite Bible scripture: *"your help cometh from the Lord"* (Psalms 121: 1-2). The lonely road he traveled to recover from his separation from God was less traveled; however, his journey taught him some valuable lessons in *the art of living.* MrJames realizes he could not have learned many of those valuable life lessons he learned on that journey in any other way. Some things can only be learned through hands-on experience and engaging in the activity.

I have never known anyone to learn to ride a bicycle or learn to roller skate without experiencing falling down a few times. Maybe you even come away with a few scrapes, some bruises, and even broken bones. For example, I recall when my son Darrell Jr. was learning to ride a skateboard; he grabbed hold of the side of my car one day as I was coasting down the street. Suddenly, we hit a rough spot in the road; I heard a thump, then a scream. Consequently, a visit to the emergency room revealed Darrell Jr. had sustained a broken wrist.

The most fundamental truth MrJames learned from his assortment of experiences is God absolutely controls *all* things, not just the *good* things of life, but literally all things of life, both heavenly and earthly. Furthermore, MrJames believes there is no such thing as a true accident; as such, nothing happens in this world by mistake—unforeseen by the creator and unintended. The Bible teaches that *"all things work together for good to them that love God, to them who are the called according to his purpose"* (Romans 8: 28). Be attentive and consciously mindful that the Bible did not say *all good things,* but it is written "all things." The author believes this means things we consider undesirable, adversarial, bad, and even unpleasant things, as well as "good" things, *all* work together for our (Christians) intended good. MrJames learned this essential truth while entangled in addictive behaviors, leaving him feeling powerless and out of control.

How do you gain unyielding confidence that God can bring peace in times of trouble? This sure confidence (faith) the author gained traveling through tragedy, chaos, confusion, times of disappointment, uncertainty, and abandonment. Consequently, from these incidents, the author learned how to embrace an unexplainable state of inner peace in tumultuous times of testing trials and tribulations.

Finally, after forty-eight months, including three rehabs, twenty-four months of relapse, active substance abuse, and chemical dependency, MrJames got some *"real help!"* He tells his story because he believes it can help give hope to those who may have a loved one caught in destructive addictive behavior patterns and those who may be struggling with issues and destructive addictive behaviors hindering stifling and controlling their lives—f.r.o.g.s. of life.

FOREWORD

For several eventful years now, I have been a friend of the Campbell family. We became church friends when they moved to Jonesboro, GA, several years ago. They appeared to be a stable, stalwart family. Little did I realize then what struggles the family was facing due to Darrell's drug addiction. They were far more stalwart and stronger than stable and secure. His wife had fled to Atlanta with their two youngest children to escape the devastating effects of her husband's addiction on their entire family.

For two different time periods, since I worked in downtown Atlanta, and I think because she trusted me not to be judgmental, I delivered packages to her husband while in two different rehabilitation centers. During one of these times, the leader of our Church men's organization, a quorum to which both Darrell and I belonged, mentioned that his wife had a bunk bed that needed to be repaired. No one was assigned, so later that week, I went to visit the Campbells' home with a bucket of tools. After this, I frequently dropped by to check on

Sister Campbell to see if there was anything else I could do for her. Needless to say, I became a trusted friend of the Campbell family. His wife spoke to me of the spirit that came into their home when Darrell would come home for the weekend from the rehab center. She was confused and did not know whether she should even have him back in her home.

Another time, following release from rehab, Darrell ended up in the county jail for driving on a suspended driver's license. I took Sister Campbell to see him. Again, she became a bit discouraged because things seemed to have been improving, but he had relapsed and made a turn toward the worst. On the way back to her home, I felt prompted by the Spirit to tell her what I felt. I told her, "Sister Campbell, Darrell is going to do as much for the people of this county as Martin Luther King Jr. has done for the nation." I felt that was true then and feel even more strongly today as I compose this.

I recall that it was not long after the second rehab center that he was back in another rehabilitation center; this was his third and final admission. I vowed that when I brought him home this time, I would offer him a supportive friendship. After that first release, I was afraid of being intrusive, and I was not certain and unaware of how much my support was needed or if needed at all. However, on the next release, I visited with Darrell once a week to offer him a hand of friendship and support. A true friendship developed as a result of the dreams, concerns, and love of the Gospel of Jesus Christ that we shared and expressed during our weekly visits. Today, I consider Darrell to be one of my very best friends.

It appears to me that Darrell did receive some *real help!* It seemed like all of a sudden; he was called to be the class instructor—teacher for the Quorum of Men we both belonged to at the Church of Jesus Christ of Latter-day Saints. He was a gifted, fabulous teacher and a delight to the Quorum members. He spoke in such a colorful, unique manner. I believe the inspiration of the Spirit prompted the Quorum Leaders to extend the call to confer this responsibility upon him.

In addition to that, and after several months of successful teaching in the Quorum, he was extended a call to serve on the High Council, a group of twelve men that presided over nine congregations of the Church of Jesus Christ of Latter-day Saints. I must admit, I was amazed and somewhat jealous that he was in the limelight to serve and assume this most noteworthy position. The president of the region had sensed spiritual greatness in Darrell and was so prompted to extend the call of this responsibility to Darrell, affectionately known throughout the Church as Brother Campbell, who *came to be known by some significant others as MrJames the LifeCoach.*

I am confident everyone will enjoy reading this account as I truly have. I had no idea of the full picture of the great challenges Bro. Campbell and his family faced and overcame. I was pleased to have been one who helped by extending a supportive hand during their time of critical need. Having attained an MS in psychology and being employed as a practicing school psychologist in public schools, I have been greatly impressed by the importance of self-*reflection* and self-introspection—the honest looking into one's inner character and soul.

Strange as it may sound, the phenomenon has been proven over time that when a person truly admits he or she has a problem, that person now has or can gain the power to start making small steps in a positive direction to overcome that difficulty. In other words, admitting weakness opens the door to power—The Power of The Creator—to strengthen weaknesses and make the needed repairs. A continual denial of the problem leaves one weak and unable to plan *and execute* an escape route. Denial of the existence of weakness is an inner lie that leads one deeper into greater weakness. Humble realization and acknowledgment of a need for help is the beginning of gaining needed power. Fasting and prayer enhance and reinforce your power.

However, as Bro. Campbell discovered, and I wholly agree, that fasting and prayer are more than candidly significant; *it is simply the most effective of all methods* to gain *real help* in overcoming persistent destructive addictive behaviors.

Once, I was in the Army National Guard and away with a tank squadron for two weeks of annual training. At summer camp, while we were out on maneuvers, there was nothing for our training section to do. I was bored out of my gourd. We stayed back in the barracks, having nothing to do. Conveniently, porno magazines were available at many of the bunks. It was too tempting; I began what turned into hours of viewing pictures and reading the unwholesome literature. The porno swiftly took all the boredom away but at an enormous inner spiritual price. Near the end of two weeks, I was feeling awful about the conscious choice I had made.

Returning home to my wife and children, I could not stop viewing and reading the magazines. In my mind, subconsciously, I could see myself slipping down a roof nearing the edge. I had sensed that once I reached the edge of the roof, I would fall quickly downward into a bottomless pit and never return. I continued viewing and reading the magazines and could not stop slipping down the roof. Thus, I could see that this became an obsessive-compulsive addiction for me!

I think because my words were empty and they were not really coming from the heart when I prayed for help, my prayers seemed to be unanswered. My mouth was speaking a lie that my head and mind did not believe, and my heart did not feel.

One day, consumed with the *desire* to refrain from this habit, a sudden inspiration came, "start fasting!" So, immediately, I skipped breakfast that day and fasted all throughout that day. My downward slide soon came to a screeching halt. My prayers began to be more meaningful and heartfelt only after relapsing a number of times and experiencing what Brother Campbell describes as the *"humiliation of disappointment."* It took me over a year of regular fasting along with prayer, regular reading of the Holy Scriptures, and other good-inspired and wholesome literature before I finally got back up to the rooftop.

So, for *real help!* I fully agree with Brother Campbell: Stop denying you have a problem; this gives you the power to begin the process of gaining increased power to change. Then, decide to add studying and reading of the Scriptures, fasting, and sincere praying to God—Our Heavenly Father, Our Creator, and Master Designer of all that exists; who stands ready to transform you into who you were created to become and put the f.r.o.g.s. in your life to death.

George Vernon "Bud" Peterson (MS Psychology)

PRELUDE

The intended purpose of making this record is to influence someone to begin to take a serious review of the patterns repeatedly illustrated and displayed in the destructive behaviors of their life and to persuade the reader to record their heartfelt impressions and thoughts. I am confident there will be some insightful perspective to come forth from your inner being as you read some of my story. Therefore, I encourage you to read and reread some of these words with a pencil and pad in hand or nearby.

At the commencement and conclusion of reading this volume, I pray that helpful insights, thoughts, and impressions will flood your mind and heart and that you will act upon those perceptions by writing them down for your future review and reflection. This volume is a record of real-life experiences reflected in the lives of millions of families. A countless number of individuals, friends, family members, and loved ones are confronted with the f.r.o.g.s. of life dilemmas in one way or another, either directly or indirectly.

The National Center on Addiction and Substance Abuse at Columbia University reported in April 2009, "a full 16 percent of the U.S. population is dependent on alcohol, nicotine, [caffeine] or other [prescription or illicit] drugs. Another 27 percent of the general population engages in [other behaviors or] the use of these substances in ways that put themselves and others at risk, including [DUI]...use and misuse of pain relievers, stimulants, and depressants. For a staggering 43 percent of the nation, then — nearly every other American — addiction and risky substance use [and other risky behaviors] are a matter of public health. Addiction is America's number one health care and health cost problem. Approximately 30 percent of our federal and state health care spending is attributable to *destructive addictive behaviors and addiction*. Across all government spending, the total financial cost is nearly $500 billion annually. [Not to mention] The human misery is incalculable" (Columbia University).

Keeping that in mind, based on my personal experiences, it is my belief that within the quiet confines of inner thoughts, impressions, and emotions lies the help many are desperately seeking from artificial and counterfeit means in vain. Many are in pursuit of an authentic *feel-good sensation* that can only be truly found and experienced by internal introspection.

The author has withheld the names of people and exact names of specific places and refrained from mentioning some particular programs, processes, and procedures in order to protect the privacy of others. Likewise, the author has not included explicit details surrounding all recorded events; no more than a drop in the ocean of experiences the addicted and non-addicted family members are encountering. Therefore, this volume is a work of fiction based on the author's personal experiences and his interpretation of the material presented.

The few hours you will need to invest as you are reviewing this work will give you only a bird's-eye view of the struggle with recovering from addictive behaviors, codependency, and chemical dependency. I once heard a wise person say, **"Experience is the best teacher,"** but another who I believe was the wiser said, **"Experience is also the most expensive."** Therefore, I conclude a smart man will learn from his own experiences; the educated man is taught and learns from books, but the foolish man learns not from his own personal experiences, not books, nor the experiences of others.

However, having considered further, I declare the wiser man learns from personal experiences, the experiences of others, and experiences he studies and reads about from books and other reliable sources. Skillful godly wisdom in the art of living, on the other hand, only comes as insight from our Creator as the result of the application of eternal principles and life lessons learned from different avenues of exposure and opportunities of experiences.

The pathway leading down the road labeled "Death to F.R.O.G.S." is paved with many such experiences. Get your shovels in your hand, in the form of pen, pencil, and paper, so we can begin to dig the F.R.O.G.S. grave. However, there are only two required commitments: a commitment to thy own self to be true and garner up the courage to be gut honest with yourself and to be relentless as you uncover pebbles, rocks, bricks, stones, and possibly some boulders while digging through your army of F.R.O.G.S, in the form of life frustrations, rejections, oppositions, grievances, sinful acts; to expose hurts, grief, disappointments, and resentments.

You, whoever You may be, will be tempted in your private thoughts to yourself, or you may actually hear yourself speak out loud that this work is intended for someone else.

Sometimes, I think to myself that *I might be talking to myself*. Maybe this message is to increase your understanding of addiction and the frogs of life in order to position you to offer some *real help!* Real Help to an addicted person in your family, or maybe a student, a co-worker, a friend, or your neighbor. This author is taking notice of the many lives lost and the families devastated by the destructive addictive behaviors of others, especially the children, who, by no fault of their own, are affected by the destructive addictive behaviors of others. After you receive *real help* to bring death to your frogs of life, the Real-Life Coach, Darrell "MrJames" Campbell, requests that you send *real help* forward in memory of the real-life experiences of Darrell James Campbell, Jr. But, please remember, directly or indirectly this message is for you, whomsoever You, The Reader, happens to be. However, keep in mind, **"I just might be talking to myself."**

1

INTRODUCTION TO AN ADDICT

Who is an Addict?

Born in the Spring of 1957 and raised by good and godly grandparents, I received much love and proper nurturing during childhood. The oldest of seven, endowed with above-average intelligence and gifted with some athletic abilities, has ambitions of becoming a doctor, business owner, and professional football player. I was a member of the Cub Scouts Boy Scouts and earned the rank of Life Scout.

I was an Honor Roll student from elementary through high school and was raised in a strong Christian environment in the home. We attended church regularly as a family; I received Christ as a youth and was first baptized at twelve years old. I remember I was well-liked and accepted by siblings, relatives, neighbors, and friends. I served as president of our freshman and sophomore classes during high school. I participated in many other academic, extracurricular, and sporting activities, and I was a member of Cub Scouts and Boy Scouts of America. I graduated in the top 20% of my high school graduating class;

however, I was married two months before my high school graduation.

I was employed for twelve years by a successful cafeteria chain, and at age twenty-five, I became one of the first African-American General Ops Managers for this fast-growing, southern-based company. I was employed as operations director and division manager of a fire and safety equipment company, operator of a commercial and residential carpet cleaning franchise, and owner/operator of a commercial and residential landscape maintenance company.

I received academic training and certification in Hotel/Restaurant Management from LaSalle Extension University; I am an alumna of Dale Carnegie's Institute of Human Relations and Public Speaking. I was educated and exposed to Self-Development Strategies and Assertiveness Training for Black Managers, and I completed Cafeteria Managers Training at the University of South Alabama. I was a licensed insurance agent and district leader in an asset management company. I served the community by serving multiple terms as PTA president and PTA Council vice-president.

I have given my time, talents, and means in service to God and my fellow man; for nearly fifty years, I have studied, read, and re-read the Holy Bible and a plethora of other sacred Scriptures. I taught Sunday school and basic Gospel principles classes for several years. I am a believer in Jesus Christ as the literal Son of God, Savior, and Redeemer of the world, and I continue my service to God as an expression of my gratitude for my miraculous deliverance from the dilemma of the f.r.o.g.s. of life and feel led to include this religious declaration.

Furthermore, having been both successful and unsuccessful

in a diverse portfolio and array of experiences, I am aware, discreet, cognitive, and always searching for opportunities to improve the life-chances for positive outcomes in the lives of those within my circles of influence. To that end, I am inclined to shout this insightful reflection to a critical mass of readers and listeners from a platform affixed to a proverbial rooftop. Albeit I haven't mentioned some of my titles, I will list a few more to aptly illuminate a life full of diversity in experiences such that I may reasonably establish, assure, assert, and be certain that someone should surely consider my comments highly credible, appropriate, timely, and applicable to present-day life challenges.

Professionally, I am a certified Life Coach-International Coaching Science Research Foundation, PLC; creator of School of Hard knocks (patreon.com/hardknocks); BS in Sociology, minor in Social Psychology; two semesters shy of MS in Applied Developmental Psychology from Clayton State University (CSU); inducted into National Society of Leadership and Success (NSLS) 2015; Sex & Drug Abuse Counseling Diploma from Stratford Career Institute 2006; awarded Outstanding Accomplishments in Sociology 2015; original research presented at Georgia Sociology Association (2013-2015), with a pending publication for Journal of Public and Professional Sociology; President of CSU Model United Nations Delegation 2013-15; Honored as Outstanding Delegate in Ecuador, Galapagos Islands 2014; served as Head Delegate in New York City 2013-2015, Czech Republic 2016; visits to Europe, Poland and Auschwitz Death Camps.

Additionally, MrJames is a former Restaurant Operations Consultant, a double franchise owner/operator of Buffalo's Southwest Cafe, and founder of Real Help! Network, Inc 2004; and co-founder of South Georgia Nonprofit Collaboration

Network (SGNCN); certified Grant Writer for Nonprofit Business Development from UGA, 2014.

I was married for over forty years, currently divorced, a father of two sons (Eagle Scouts), a daughter attending Columbus State University, and three adorable granddaughters: Trinity the Genius (15), Mariah the Thoughtful (10), Morgan the Enquirer (8). I have enjoyed some of the best of times, things, and experiences in this world, as well as some of the most trying and challenging. This Includes choice relationships with family, in-laws, and relatives, and a full quiver of friendships, more than I can count on my fingers and toes. In a co-parenting partnership with my wife, together we financially, emotionally, physically, and spiritually provided for our three children from conception and infancy through adolescence and on into adulthood.

As the young man's story began and with his limited understanding of drug abuse, addiction, relapse, and recovery, he, like many others, without hesitation would have said the above description does not fit the characteristic profile of a person most of us would initially and readily identify as an addict. However, the described young man is in the process of recovering from a chemical-dependency drug addiction that almost cost him everything, including his wife, his family, material possessions, sentimental properties, heirlooms, and almost his life.

The following is a partial listing of some titles an addict may be labeled and answers to traveling on life's journey: Husband (Wife), Father (Mother), Brother (Sister), Uncle (Aunt), Niece (Nephew), and even Preacher (Pastor), Spiritual Leader, Teacher, Doctor, Lawyer, and child, just to mention a few. Take notice that this young man was a business owner/operator, employed as an operations manager, division manager, general manager, and other middle- to upper-level management and leadership positions.

Do not be deceived by educational/academic accomplishments, social status, positions, or socioeconomic income levels. These subsequent pages will detail some of his stories; he shares his story because he believes some truths that he learned on his journey through Damascus, Hades, and Gethsemane were revealed to him. Returning from the abyss of destruction, he explains these truths within his story. He further believes these truths, when observed, can serve as REAL HELP to those others seeking real recovery from the f.r.o.g.s. of life. You will find, however, numerous similarities in his story, not much different from all others suffering and struggling with this chemical-dependency addiction.

Finally, with an abundance of gratitude, after nearly fifty months of use, abuse, and addiction, including eighteen months of in-house residential rehabs, and after several relapse episodes, this grateful young man finally got some REAL HELP to put the f.r.o.g.s. in his life to death. Now endowed with skillful godly wisdom, this young man is enlightened and becoming a transformed man: from a hopeless, helpless addict to real recovery. Nonetheless, this young man cautions the reader and all others that chemical dependency addiction and destructive addictive behavior is no respecter of a person: "cunning, baffing, powerful" and can be fatal. (A.A. 58-59).

Furthermore, those so infected will live a life in jails, hospitals, rehabs, and other institutions, and if not treated, chemical dependency addiction will lead to an unfulfilled eternal destiny and, ultimately, physical death. Addiction will and can affect paupers or kings, natives, Americans or foreigners, Caucasians or African-Americans, male or female, and young or older; it truly does not discriminate. Education is the most effective defense against this thief of the night. The close, sincerely caring family members of those *Building Up Drug Dependency* (B.U.D.D) and other caring, loving family members must become knowledgeable in the treatment process for recovery in order to minimize the negative effects of chemical-dependency addiction and destructive addictive behaviors on other family members and mitigate its effect on the body, mind, and spirit of the endangered person.

Some people consider addictions to be simply bad habits that can be conquered by willpower alone, but many people become so dependent on a behavior or a substance that they no longer see how to abstain from it. They lose perspective and a sense of other priorities in their lives. Nothing matters more than satisfying their desperate need. When they try to abstain, they experience powerful physical, psychological, and emotional cravings. As they habitually make wrong choices, they find their ability to choose the right diminished or restricted.

There are many kinds of addictions, and it is difficult for someone who has one of these serious addictions to change because **some of them are mind-altering**. A recent article on addiction said, **"In the brains of addicts, there is reduced activity in the prefrontal cortex, where rational thought can override impulse behavior."** Michael D. Lemonick and Alice Park, "The Science of Addiction," Time, July 16, 2007, 44.

The fasciculus *retroflexus*

Science News... *from universities, journals, and other research organizations*

Nicotine Causes Selective Degeneration In Brain, UCLA Neuroscientists Report

ScienceDaily (Nov. 10, 2000) — Nicotine causes degeneration in a region of the brain that affects emotional control, sexual arousal, REM sleep, and seizures, UCLA neuroscientists report in the current issue of the journal Neuropharmacology.

"Nicotine causes the most selective degeneration in the brain that I have ever seen, " said UCLA neuroscientist Gaylord Ellison, a professor of psychology and member of UCLA's Brain Research Institute. "Only one tract of the brain is affected."

The part of the brain that is affected by nicotine is called fasciculus retroflexus, which has two halves. In previous research conducted over more than two decades, Ellison's research team has shown that such drugs as amphetamines, cocaine, and ecstasy damage one-half of fasciculus retroflexus. In the journal Neuropharmacology and at the Society for Neuroscience's annual meeting in New Orleans this month, Ellison's research team reports for the first time that nicotine causes degeneration in the other half of fasciculus retroflexus. The neuroscientists further report that the drugs that damage one-half of fasciculus retroflexus do not damage the other half that nicotine affects.

"Our findings suggest that this (fasciculus retroflexus) is the brain's weak link for stimulant addictive drugs," Ellison said. "This tract is affected more by chronic drug use than any other tract in the brain."

"It seems likely that fasciculus retroflexus is linked to drug addiction and relapse," Ellison said. "In chronic smokers, this tract may well play a major role in the addiction to nicotine."

Fasciculus retroflexus is a pathway that emerges from the brain's habenula, which is above the thalamus. (The habenula is the chief relay nucleus of the descending dorsal die cephalic conduction system.) **This pathway is a part of the brain that is not well understood.** The researchers administered nicotine to rats for five days through a mini-pump inserted under their skin. At high doses of nicotine, the degeneration was almost complete in the pathway.

"We initially gave relatively high doses of nicotine and then reduced it to a dose that induces plasma levels of nicotine in rats comparable to those of two-pack-a-day smokers," Ellison said. "Even at this much lower dose, we still found degeneration in the tract. We measured the degeneration and found that the larger the dose, the more damage." Ellison's research team includes his UCLA graduate students Janice Carlson, Brian Armstrong, and Robert Switzer of NeuroScience Associates. Ellison has studied the effects of drugs on the brain for more than 20 years. His research is funded by the National Institute of Drug Abuse and the Tobacco-Related Disease Research Program, which is funded by California's tobacco tax.

University Of California, Los Angeles (2000, November 10). Nicotine Causes Selective Degeneration In Brain, UCLA Neuroscientists Report. *ScienceDaily*. Retrieved April 6, 2012, from http://www.sciencedaily.com **/releases/2000/11/00111007**

2

JOURNEY THROUGH ADDICTION

Born in the Spring of 1957 and raised by godly grandparents, the young man received much love and nurturing during childhood. He was the oldest child of (7) seven, endowed with above-average intelligence and athletic abilities. He was an Honor Roll student, raised in a strong Christian environment, including active family participation in church. He received Christ and was first baptized at age twelve. He was well and accepted by friends, classmates, neighbors, siblings, and relatives. He served as freshman and sophomore class president during his high school years. He participated in many other academic and extracurricular activities, including a Cub Scout and a Boy Scout, and attained the rank of Life Scout.

The young man graduated in the top 20% of his high school graduating class, ranked #64 of 319, and before his graduation in 1975, he married a co-worker and class member from the 1974 high school graduating class. Employed at the company for over twelve years during the Civil Rights Era, the young man became one of the growing southern-based company's first Black General Operations Managers at the age of 25. Additionally, he has enjoyed leadership employment positions such as operations director, division manager, owner-operator of a landscape maintenance company, as well as founder owner/operator of other companies.

He received certification and training in Hotel/Restaurant Management from LaSalle Extension University. He completed Dale Carnegie's Human Relations & Public Speaking Course, Graduate of Self-Development Strategies, Assertiveness Training for Black Managers, and Cafeteria Managers training from the University of South Alabama. He is a former licensed insurance and asset manager. He diligently served his fellow man, giving of time, talent, and means in devoted service to God, for nearly 15 years. He has served on executive boards of local PTA councils and other civic organizations. He has read and reread the Holy Bible and other sacred Scriptures, teaching Sunday school and Basic Gospel Doctrine and Principles classes. He served (5) five years in a local ministerial congregational leadership role as an advisor and administrator. He is knowledgeable about religion and believes in the reality of the birth, life, death, and resurrection of Jesus Christ as Savior and Redeemer of the world. He has experienced and enjoyed the best of the best of life, including a wife and three terrific children. He strives to be meek and not boisterous, soft-spoken, not overbearing or demanding. Co-parenting with his wife, they raised their three children into adulthood, two sons and a daughter, and celebrated the bestowal of the highly revered Eagle Scout Award upon both of their sons. Their daughter has provided them the opportunity to raise the first three of many expected grandchildren.

With a limited understanding of addiction, the aforementioned description does not fit the typical characteristic profile of a person most of us would readily identify as an addict. This young man, however, is in the process of recovering from a drug addiction that cost him his wife, his family, and almost his life. Furthermore, he experienced the loss of many material and sentimental possessions, self-respect, dignity, and the respect of others.

Following a combined total of forty months of on-again and off-again active addiction and sixteen months of on-again and off-again relapsing, including three residential recovery rehab programs (1996-2000), finally, the young man got some *real-help.*

The subsequent account will detail some of his story. There are some truths revealed and explained within his story that can serve as a help to others seeking real recovery.

You will find, however, that his story differs not much from most all others suffering and still struggling with chemical dependency and destructive addictive behaviors. Addiction is no respecter of persons; it is, it will be, and it can be fatal. Moreover, it can and will affect paupers, kings, natives, Americans, foreigners, white or black, male or female, and young or older; it truly does not discriminate.

However, education can be the most effective defense and, ultimately, the most effective offense against this thief of the night. The chemically dependent addict and caring non-addicted family members must become knowledgeable and effectively educated in providing evidence-based assistance to their loved ones. This will help to minimize the physical, emotional, psychological, sociological, financial, spiritual, and mental effects on the body, mind, spirit, and consciousness of extended family members, as well as provide encouragement for endangered persons. These words come into his mind as the young man reflects on that first night:

The very people I loved,
Are the same people I hurt the most?
The things I said I would not do,
Are the very things I did?
The places I said I would not go,
Are the exact same places I went?
I wish there were
Some wonderful places:
Called the land of beginning again;
Where all our mistakes,
And all our heartaches, all of our
Poor selfish grief,
Could be dropped like a shabby old coat
At the door, and never be put on again. (author unknown)

That first night in February 1996, when the young man was offered that crack pipe, has a permanent memory path etched into his brain. That night, different from all other nights, was the night the young man did not possess enough strength of character to "just say no" after having enjoyed fifteen years of total abstinence from drugs, alcohol, coffee, tobacco, and any and all other mind-altering substances.

Feeling particularly distressed that night, the young man can recall throbbing feelings of hopelessness, helplessness, frustration, and confusion relating to life and the future of his family. As such, his feelings of loneliness, abandonment, frustration, disappointment, and humiliation were permeating all areas of his now-troubled life.

During these feelings of impending hopelessness, helplessness, and frustration, it was as if the young man saw a picture in his mind's eye. It was a frog in a pot of water, and he could hear his grandmother saying to him, as she had said so many times throughout his life, *"Remember the frog."*

The young man was totally disappointed with his progress in life after changing employers. Even now, reflecting upon those days, he can still remember the anxious, frustrated feelings of being stuck in a helpless situation. Similar to frustrations experienced by a driver of an eighteen-wheeler on a crowded dead-end street, stuck in a traffic jam, trying desperately to turn his ring around so he could get out of there and back on the road.

For several years, the young man had been trying to regain his self-confidence from the negative effects of occupational-related business decisions and other entrepreneurial experiences. His lack of authentic expression of his innermost thoughts and feelings to his wife and his failure to share his feelings with anyone else who was significant in his life unknowingly opened the door of entry for unresolved inner conflict, cognitive dissonance, confusion, and the onslaught of a barrage of negative detrimental and damaging self-talk. A silent inner dialog was going on between his ears and behind his eyes. An unspoken conversation that included blaming others and finger-pointing.

Additionally, the young man felt betrayed by individuals that he thought truly cared for him and his family's welfare. This frame of mind, fueled by a negative self-talk that refused to accept any personal responsibility, had given birth to a state of anger and resentment that only increased his inner turmoil. Having been frantically kicking, trying to stay afloat through a decade of struggles, trials, and disappointments, the young man was already on the brink of exhaustion. Therefore, his distorted perception of betrayal, levied against his family, was the straw that broke the proverbial camel's back. This perceived threat was the spark that ignited the inner turmoil and conflict into a raging fire, giving place for f.r.o.g.s. in his life that would finally beat the young man down and further wound his now fragile self-esteem and self-image.

It is apparent to him, as he reflects back on the memories of those days, long before the birth of his daughter in 1986, that he had been fighting to keep his sanity for nearly ten years. There were times when he had been uplifted and encouraged, but repeatedly, time and time again, he would be deceived, exploited, let down by those close to him, and would experience disappointment and despair.

The young man continued to kick and fight; he refused to stop and give up altogether. However, over the years, he had compromised certain moral territory and ethical values. He was on the slippery slope of setting aside some basic foundational principles of the Gospel, doctrines, and beliefs, even though there had been many years of sincere devotion and commitment to the Church and its teachings. Under the persistent pressure of the f.r.o.g.s. of life, this time, the young man faltered, failed the test, and succumbed to an attitude consistent with throwing in the towel and giving up the fight. Therefore, owing to poor judgment, wrong choices, the dilemma of f.r.o.g.s. and the weight from the stresses of life, figuratively, the young man blew out his head gasket, busted his radiator, and busted his oil pan. Consequently, the young man buckled under the pressure, and sometime in 1994, the young man **started losing his faith**, his confidence, and his determination to endure.

Starting in 1987-1994, the young man was just working, working, and working, trying to stay afloat, but the f.r.o.g.s. of life continued. He filed for bankruptcy, his vehicle was repossessed, his car engine blew, he became more and more judgmental, and he lost respect for some local church members and began to harbor feelings of unforgiveness and resentment toward his spouse and others.

Facing major health consequences and concerns relating to the premature birth of their son Devin in 1993, the young man began to feel increasing stress from life's pressing problems and the uncertainty of situations that were beyond his ability to change, influence, or control.

I remember feeling helpless; all my dreams and ambitions were lost, and the future seemed **more and more hopeless.** That same year, our oldest son had graduated from high school and gone into the military. Although I consented to his decision, it went against my core beliefs and expectations for him, creating inner discontent, cognitive dissonance, and a desire to disconnect from the painful construct of my reality. This decision to enter the military created conflict between Angelia and me, and from then on, she would occasionally throw this up in my face.

I remember feeling, based on my desires for what I thought was best, I had not properly guided my son. As his father, the young man began to realize that this decision contributed to Junior acting out behavior contrary to his spiritual teachings and confessed beliefs. Junior had become sexually active. We had spent several years planning a certain path for him, but as his father, this young man had not insistently demanded it be followed, and he still remembers feeling confused, angry, frustrated, and inadequate as a father. This young man remembers those feelings of failure every time he is reminded of this decision. However, he never expressed these feelings, isolating himself more from family and friends, and for the first time in nearly fifteen years, he started distancing himself from church friends.

Feeling a bit better about finances, avoiding relationships by consuming himself with work, things were deceitfully looking better. However, internally, he was feeling his all-time worst; in the fall of 1995, he was appropriately released from church leadership responsibilities, and his church attendance and participation decreased for the first time in fifteen years. This young man acknowledges that he gradually fell into a state of **self-pity, depression, loneliness, confusion, and frustration.**

During the month of February 1996, on the way home from work one night, he gave someone a ride. He distinctly remembers he was feeling especially hopeless, helpless, frustrated, and abandoned. Recollecting and reflecting upon that night, the young man bears in mind that when he was offered that pipe, he took it because, at the time, he did not possess the strength of character nor the sense of self-worth necessary at that moment to just say no!

"And as they say... the rest is history."

That was twenty-five years ago, subsequent to fifteen years of Church membership, many hours of study, fervent prayer, and solemn meditation, congruent with the constant pressure and continuous barrage of diverse temptations: tests, trials, and tribulations. Yes, that night, the young man accepted a hit from that pipe, and immediately, he realized he had embarked into some unknown area of experience. It created within him an artificial but seemingly realistic burst of energy and excitement, but a counterfeit *feel-good sensation* of extreme pleasure, followed by overwhelming calm and relaxation. The young man admits honestly, however, that he really only felt that intense *feel-good sensation* and extreme experience of pleasure, followed by a seemingly overwhelming sense of relaxation, but only, and possibly twice. However, in reality, he may have only experienced that intense feeling during that initial encounter. From that time forward, the young man describes his journey through addiction as a continuous chasing after an elusive counterfeit *feel-good sensation*. He was chasing after those feelings for months and years to come, only to occasionally come close but never to complete inner satisfaction. The young man recognized he was always left with the feeling that the next hit would be the one, and then you would be finished. But the counterfeit sensation was never enough.

The young man is almost brought to tears, even now, as he remembers and realizes just how consumed he allowed his pursuit of the *feel-good sensation* to progress into his conscious thoughts and behavior. His family is caught-up in the addiction whirlwind and headed for a train wreck, but finally, his family is fed up and leaves him all alone.

Nineteen months later, after that first hit, one Saturday morning, a police officer knocked on the window of the young man's van. He was preparing to get high. Just before the knock, the young man had experienced a strange feeling of calmness around him. In the consciousness of the calmness, somehow communicating, not audible, but in reality, and in essence, it said to him that something good, something better than good, even very good, was about to happen. For that short moment in the construct of the young man's reality, all feelings of abandonment, hopelessness, helplessness, shame, fear, frustration, and confusion had left him. All the young man could recall is that he saw, not with his eyes, but more like in a conscious sense of awareness; he became consciously attuned to the reality of his immediate surroundings; it appeared that the area around him became illuminated brighter, almost a radiant light.

The young man experienced a brief moment of peace, calm, and complete silence. As he looked up and around, a police officer began knocking on the window of his van. He never asked my name nor for my license or anything. It was a male and a female officer, and their faces seemed as though they were familiar. The officer asked him questions about his family and his addiction, destroyed the drugs he had in his possession, and told him to go and get some help. This encounter with the officers lasted about five minutes or so. Those few minutes, along with his experience a few moments before, were the beginning of the young man's decision to change from active addiction and enter into the process of recovery. Even though spiritually, he knew something in reality had happened to him, he was still in the grips of his out-of-control addictive behavior and pursuit of the counterfeit *feel-good sensation.*

The young man had prayed deep within himself the night before for God to put him on the right path and show him the way back to soundness of mind and sanity. This event brought him a real sense of awareness of the all-consuming nature of chemical dependency and the reality of his addiction. The young man knew that the addicted person was not him; in essence, he was not himself. And that shocking truth catapults him into a connection with reality that eventually coalesces with his courage, bringing forth the tenacity to make a good decision for change. On that day, feeling hopeless, helpless, discontent, and abandoned, in the early fall of 1997, wallowing around with the f.r.o.g.s of life, the young man was at the lowest point of his entire life. He was feeling humiliated, ashamed, and frustrated, experiencing loneliness, confusion, hopelessness, helplessness, and abandonment. He came to realize that he was indeed suffering from a separation from God. He had, however, given considerable thought about his next step, and he was fully certain of his spiritual experience,

As the days progressed, he refrained from making any quick decisions. He was confused, uncomfortable, and concerned for his family. Therefore, he made a decision (not completely on his own) mostly because of the family circumstances. He got a job, but it was not the right thing to do. The money in hand indirectly triggers the young man into a relapse, leading him back into active addiction. A few days later, he entered Rehab #1, a Christian in-house program.

The young man arrived at the Ranch feeling worthless, deserted, humiliated, ashamed, and frustrated, feeling real loneliness, hopelessness, helplessness, abandonment, and confusion. He was so heartbroken that the only comfort that came to him was from his knowing and believing that God could and would care for and protect his family. Before leaving, he sincerely asked God to provide for his family's needs, and he turned them over to HIS care, to the care of God. He accepted the fact that he could not care for them. At that moment, it was as if he could hear his grandmother saying to him, as she had said so many times throughout his life… *"All you can do is all you can do, and trust God to do the rest."*

3

FROG IN THE MILK

While in a state of reflection, during the time he was experiencing his *real-life* feelings of frustration, it was as if he could see, in his mind's eye, a frog in a huge tub of milk. At some point, it sounded like he heard his grandmother again. She was saying, as she had said to him so many times during his life, *"Remember the frog."*

Intriguingly, the young man began to remember a story his grandmother had told him about a farmer. The farmer had some fresh milk from his cows, and he had been busy churning butter in a big tub of milk.

Suddenly, the farmer had to leave the milk tub sitting unattended for a while as he rushed off to go inside. It was about this same time that along came a frog, jumping and hopping its way through. Haphazardly, the frog was not paying much attention to its surroundings, just freely jumping all around as frogs normally do. One way or another, unexpectedly, the frog jumps and, to its surprise, ends up smack dab in the middle of the farmer's tub of milk. Just as the frog rises to the surface of the tub of milk, the farmer returns and notices the frog kicking and struggling as hard as it can to jump out of the tub of milk.

As disappointed as the farmer was about the tub of milk being ruined by the frog, he was not so anxious as to hurriedly rescue the toad from its predicament. From a position nearby, the farmer watches the frog struggling in the milk for a time. The farmer began thinking of the poor little frog, kicking and kicking just as hard as it could. Trying desperately to free itself and get out of the tub of milk.

On a few occasions, as the farmer continued to **observe**, the frog would manage to get to the side of the tub but just could not maneuver itself with enough strength and force to jump out. The frog would sink to the bottom of the tub and attempt to push off the bottom, but the tub is too deep, and the frog is only able to barely leap above the surface of the milk. Unfortunately, for the frog, the surface of the milk is well below the rim of the tub. This old frog in the milk, **knowing what he knows**, knows he must keep trying because it seems as though the only way out is to jump out. The frog decides within itself it will keep on kicking, kicking, and kicking until it comes to night exhaustion, nearly depleting all its strength. Then, the frog would drop to the bottom of the tub of milk to rest momentarily.

The farmer, thus far having been quite amused by the efforts of the little frog, decides to rescue the determined little frog the next morning. The farmer left the frog in the tub for the evening and through the night to see what would happen, intending to rescue the frog in the morning.

The frog continues, kicking harder and harder, trying to kick hard enough to propel itself up over the rim of the tub, but to no avail. The frog was in a kicking fight for its life. The only choice for the frog that seemed apparent, even though it was not working, was for the frog to keep on keeping on. The presently unfruitful effort of kicking was the only hope for freeing itself. Therefore, for the rest of the evening and through the darkness of night, the frog continues the ritual of kicking, kicking, and then kicking to exhaustion, dropping to the bottom, resting, and continuing to kick some more. At the point of almost total exhaustion, almost ready to give up on ever getting out of the tub of milk, the frog settled on the bottom of the tub, looking around for an extended period of inactivity and **reflection**.

Suddenly, the frog begins to look around at its surroundings; for the first time, the frog notices that there are some lumps in the milk on the bottom of the tub. The frog also noticed as it was kicking, kicking, and kicking, the lumps were moving around, and some of the lumps would even float up to the surface. The frog had only been focused on what he thought was the only way out. It had not noticed, nor had the frog given any thought to what was lying around. The frog had jumped into a tub of buttermilk.

Now, as he was kicking, the frog had become aware of the lumps, and the frog began to kick until the lumps moved from the bottom and floated up to the surface. Such that the lumps began to pile up until the frog had built a mound out of the lumps. The frog continued kicking until the mound of lumps was sufficiently firm enough to hold its weight. Just as night was turning to day, the morning sunlight began to break through, and the vacating darkness was displaced by daylight. The dawn of a new day was beginning to come forth, and the frog was found seated on the newly constructed mound of lumps.

The frog was now calm and resting from its long,

exhausting night of fervent kicking and jumping. As daybreak arrived, the farmer anxiously returned to the tub of milk to examine the fate of the frog. Just as the farmer arrived and the morning light began to peak through, the farmer was amazed to catch a glimpse of the big frog just as it was leaping over the rim of the tub. The frog had left behind a mound of lumps of butter in the tub of milk.

It was as if the young boy could hear his grandmother softly saying, as she had said so many times throughout his life… **"Keep on keeping on; help is on the way, and it is usually closer than you think."** The young man vows to always remember the frog in the milk and to keep on keeping on. Therefore, the young man concludes: **after you have done your best, all you can do is all you can do, and then that is all you can do; just trust God for the rest.**

Therefore, when you find yourself in a hard place, do the best you can and all you can to come out of that place. However, after you have done all you can do, that is all you can do; then you must be willing to trust God to do the rest. Nevertheless, whatever you do, do not give up and quit. Just keep on kicking and kicking, and keep on kicking, even though the darkness of the night, because who knows what the morning may bring. Keep on keeping on and do not quit; help is not far away. Remember the frog in the milk.

4

WRITTEN LIFE-INVENTORY

THIS CHAPTER IS DEDICATED TO: TWELVE-STEP RECOVERY PRINCIPLE

Once upon a time in the small, deep southern town of Prichard, Alabama, in the approaching days of the autumn of 1971, a young teenage boy was sitting in his ninth-grade classroom at school. The teacher had received an urgent message from the office that the young boy needed to come home due to an emergency. When he arrived home, where he lived with two adopted sisters and his grandmother, she was not there, but several other family members were.

The young boy's sixty-nine-year-old grandmother, Willie Inez Campbell, was really his legally adopted mother. She was described as a very industrious person—quiet, kind, soft-spoken, and stayed mostly to herself. She was loved and well-respected by her brothers, sisters, and other relatives. Affectionately, she was loved and revered by her children, her children's children and great-grandchildren. She was a well-liked neighbor in the community, willing to share what she had with the less fortunate. Her mother, the young boy's great-grandmother, Pastoria Mosley Beasley, was born on 12 June

1880. He had been told she was a descendant of the Black Creek Indians of Central Alabama. His grandmother was known by those who knew her well as Inez; she was born on 22 Sept 1902 in Evergreen, Conecuh, County, Alabama. She had taught him to cook, sew, iron, wash clothes, grocery shop, and clean house, as well as how and when to plant vegetables. She loved flowers and taught him to grow and care for them. She also taught him to properly can and preserve all kinds of fruits and vegetables for later consumption (canning preserves). He learned from her a deep-rooted philosophy of: *"All you can do is all you can do, if that is your best, trust God to do the rest."*

His grandfather, Richard Norris Campbell, who was really his legally adopted father, had passed away in 1963. The passing of the young man's grandparents, especially his grandmother's passing, became the most traumatic event etched in the memory of the childhood of this young man. When he was called home from school that day, it was soon thereafter that that day truly became the saddest day of his young life.

His life suddenly became more perplexing, even more so than the trauma he had experienced the year before as one of the first students of integrated public schools in the South. Nonetheless, the inhumane, horrific, and consequential experiences of court-ordered and law-enforced public school integration were shocking, distressful, and tragic. Particularly, this time was traumatic for children in their early formative years of influence. As it was, during 1970-71, the young man was just an eighth-grade middle school student. However, mentally and from a psychological perspective, the effect of those experiences on him was not as bewildering and traumatizing as the death of his grandparent. Furthermore, this young man's primary caregiver and adult socializing role model, for most of his life, had been his grandmother.

Upon arriving home, he was informed his grandmother was not there. She had a heart attack at the house and had been pronounced dead on the way to the hospital. She transitioned to this earthly existence on 23 Sept 1971. She had celebrated her birthday with family and enjoyed a surprise birthday party just the day before. Present at the party were her five living birthed children, three adopted children, her thirty-two grandchildren, her nine great-grandchildren, and many other relatives who visited. Some of her birthday cake from her party, the young man recalls, remained untouched in the refrigerator for several weeks.

The young man's heartfelt feelings of devastation lingered. As he reflects on those memories, he remembers his feelings of being abandoned and alone. He became more frustrated, confused, and frightened and a great deal more uncertain about life than he had ever been before. He remembers emotional sentiments of blame and wishing he had been home, suggesting to himself that maybe then she would not have died.

He loved his grandmother so very much; she had taught him to take care of himself and prepared him for his world ahead. He carries in his heart vivid memories of rubbing her feet and hands to ease her old-aged pains of arthritis or rheumatism. He was not sure if she or her doctors were certain which it was she had at the time. He can still hear her saying, "Old man Arthur road me all night last night," as she greeted the young boy on many mornings. He would then say, "Madea," a slang word for mother dear, "why didn't you wake me up so I could come to rub your feet," and then she would give some kind reply.

Madea's death ushered in a new beginning and a world of change for the young boy, who would soon be fifteen years old.

Through the years, he had developed some skills and possessed better-than-average abilities playing football, baseball, and golf. He carries a vivid recollection of missing the opening game of his high school football experience because the game was on the exact same day as his grandmother's funeral.

The young man and his thirteen-year-old biological sister, who was also legally adopted by the grandparents, continued to live in the same house they had grown up in. This served to provide a sense of stability in the changing world of his new life. He and his sister Glenda's birth mother, Iola Campbell Conner, and her husband, Willie James Conner, moved into the house together.

However, the other legally adopted sister, who was an eleven-year-old cousin named Jacquelyn, moved home with her birth mother, who was his mother's youngest sister. The three of them had grown up together, with their grandmother as their nurturing mother, as literal brothers and sisters all of their young lives.

Therefore, the young man and his sister were now living with their married biological mother, who had their other three sisters and brother living in the house with them. Their other siblings were Karl Leon Bolls (9), Mamie Willena Conner (7), Alison Bolls (6), and Lynette Marie Conner (5). They also had another brother, who had been adopted by their mother's brother, who was their Uncle Earl Campbell. The other brother's name was Earl Campbell (11). This was actually a family secret that was not supposed to be widely known. There it was; suddenly, all eight of them were living under the same roof for the first time. However, he still recalls the lasting feelings of being abandoned, frustrated, confused, and all alone, albeit now he is amongst a house full of people.

During this already distressing and traumatic time, he was

also being confronted directly, face to face with racism, prejudices, and discrimination. Matriculating middle school in conjunction with the first year of court-enforced public school integration in the South was a chaotic time of sociological transition. It was a truly traumatic period filled with real-life daily drama intense life-forming, and life-changing experiences. This young man, along with many other students, was involved in and was confronted with several incidents of discrimination, racism, prejudices, and injustice. As such, he and many other students had been suspended more than once.

As a consequence of the tension, atmosphere, and fears of the time, a story was told about an incident in the hallway at his middle school. There was a lone teenage Caucasian student walking through the school hallway. Just as the Caucasian kid turned a corner, he found himself face to face with a lone teenage African-American student, simultaneously turning the corner in the hallway but walking in opposing directions toward each other. Both teenagers were subconsciously convinced they were in grave danger. Both were terrified at the mere sight of the other and became victims, reacting to the negative social construct of each student's reality.

The young man believes the negative conditioning from their environment perpetuates both teens' reactions. Negative, biased, and prejudiced conditioning by embedded teaching of hatred, intolerance, and bigotry. The young man comes to realize that negative persuasions and influences were being planted by significant people into the lives, values, and belief systems of students. These significant influential people were sometimes parents, teachers, older siblings, relatives, friends, fellow students, police officers, media, etc.

Consequently, the Caucasian student was absolutely so terrified he suddenly turned around and started running frantically away from the African-American student. The African-American student sprints off running after the Caucasian student. While running, trying to get away, the Caucasian student panics and runs into some kind of closed door. Somehow, a glass window is shattered and broken, and the glass cuts the Caucasian student badly.

Juxtaposition the young man, the Caucasian teen, and the African-American teen, and it will be found each had been inundated with similar negative experiential conditioning in the weeks prior to the incident. There were several incidents involving Caucasian police that were witnessed by the young man. Police officers would be watching while other Caucasian adults were throwing rocks, bricks, glass, sticks, and chains at him and other African-American teens as they walked through their Caucasian neighborhood in order to get to their assigned school.

They both had witnessed fights and beatings with sticks and chains on the way to school and on the way home again. They both had witnessed friends being jumped on and beaten several mornings by groups of Caucasian and African-American students retaliating in school hallways. The fear and instilled hatred between both groups of people caused negative, violent, and malicious actions to surface within both groups, sometimes at the mere sight of one another.

The sadness of that incident, however, as the story is told, was the fact that if there had been two normal, young, unbiased Caucasian and African-American teens, there would not have been an incident. The truth is, if they had been allowed to just be *kids* without the negative biases and influences, there probably would have been no incident.

Over the years, this young man became very aware of the effects his environment has on his reactions to issues in life.

This developed within him a sense of inevitable obligation, on his part, to form opinions of individuals based as much as possible on points that he had considered about a person independently as individuals, not just blindly accepting other person's opinions, labeling, and stereotyping of one another.

Before leaving middle school, he learned, from that tragic accident, to be respectful of all people, seeing them as he saw and understood himself. He learned that people, situations, the environment, and the people around us can influence us all. Rarely do we act entirely on our own, but more often than we care to admit, we are simply reacting or being acted upon. This has led the young man to a life philosophy based on generally trusting all persons initially until sufficient reason is given to treat them otherwise.

Sometime during that 1970-71 school year, the young man met a girl, and they became the best of friends. He had not been much interested in girls, but their friendship slowly progressed into an affectionate friendship with lots of talking and sharing. Eventually, after admitting their feelings to one another, their relationship continued its course for around three years. The young man is now pleased to announce that never, not even once, did this affair express itself through sexual intercourse. However, admittedly, as he recalls and reflects, they engaged in some heavy petting. Such that had it continued, they were on a slippery path. Nonetheless, intimately, they both had shared their deeply rooted desire for their wedding night to be consummated as a virgin for whom they would marry.

Madea's death surely ushered in new beginnings for the young boy, an ongoing world of change. He was on the football team at school, and his girl was a cheerleader. He remembers missing their opening game of the season because it was scheduled the same day, in the evening, of his grandmother's funeral. He remembers looking out the window of the funeral car as they passed the stadium where the game was about to be played. He was feeling alone, abandoned, frustrated, disappointed, and humiliated in all areas of his life. During that intense moment of reflection, recollection, and review, it was as if he could hear his grandmother saying to him, as she had said so many times throughout his life... *"Remember the frog."*

As the young man continued adjusting to *the art of living* in the life situation with his birth mother, he began feeling more and more frustrated. Primarily, there were too many extreme changes. Such as it was, the hardest and most demanding adjustment was tolerating the behavior of his alcoholic stepfather. The stepfather's *destructive, addictive behavior,* when under the influence of alcohol, usually led to harsh acts of violence against his mother. His grandparents were not drinkers; his birth mother was not a drinker.

However, there were a good number of sociable, party-going personalities among the young man's relatives. Nevertheless, he had not been exposed firsthand to the type of violent and humiliating behavior associated with alcoholism. Admittedly, there were some alcoholics among his many relatives; the young man's real exposure to that behavior was very limited, especially the violence associated with alcoholism. However, the young man was well aware and knew his mother had been hospitalized more than once because of the stepfather's violence.

Consequently, all the other children had lived in continual fear, shame, humiliation, and embarrassment. Likewise, the young man is becoming more and more embarrassed by the situation and very much ashamed. He soon stops talking, starts isolating himself, and hiding his feelings within. Entering the tenth grade, he changed his interests, and plans for his future life focus were skewed and altered. He stopped pursuing sports, athletics, fishing, camping, and other nature-related outdoor hobbies.

He was losing his motivation and self-directed drive to aspire to the academic heights he had set as goals for himself. Furthermore, he continued to grapple with his feelings of being alone, abandoning all areas of his now troubled and chaotic life.

PERSONAL OUTLINE HE USED

TO BEGIN THE 4TH STEP

LIFE HISTORY BULLET POINTS

--Tragic sudden loss of my grandfather

--Life with a grandmother instead of the birth mother

--Absence of father figure

--Separation from brother and sisters

--Tragic sudden loss of grandmother—adopted mother

--Sudden change in the whole world (unstable)

--Life with new parents

--Life with other siblings

--Feelings of abandonment

--Feelings of rejection by father

--Searching for the father I never had

--Racism, integration, and prejudices

--Filling loneliness with female companionship

--Loss of self-respect and self-esteem

--Reduced focus on education

--Start working

--Move out on own at 17

--Losing self-interests

--Intro to marijuana

--Unplanned pregnancy

--Married at 18
--Loss of trust in relationships
--Feelings of not fitting in
--Real feelings not expressed
--More frustration and loneliness
--More rejection, confusion
--Tragic death of birth mother
--Stepfather in prison
--Orphan siblings move in
--Household conflicts increase
--Disappointed by those in authority over me
--Followed the path of least resistance
--Judging personality before principles
--Punishment and guilt for sinful behavior
--Deny feelings by avoiding sensitive issues
--Loss of stable female companionship
--Feelings of loss of love or absence of caring
--Self-isolation
--Incomplete cycles of grief
--Absence of fear
--Needing to feel affection through intimacy
--Feelings of failure
--Feelings of hopelessness and helplessness

5

THE COOKED FROG

During this time of feeling shameful, worthless, humiliated, frustrated, lonely, hopeless, helpless, deserted, abandoned, and confused, it was as if he could see, in his mind's eye, a cooked frog in a pot of water and he could hear his grandmother saying as she had said so many times through his life.... *"Just remember the frog."*

His grandmother told him a story about a farmer who caught a very large frog using a homemade trap he had placed in the water at the creek pond. The big frog had eluded the farmer for a long time. The farmer really desired to have some tasty bullfrog stew; therefore, he quickly placed the trap in the water so that it was difficult to detect in the murky water of the creek pond. This was the farmer's lucky day, and he was elated with excitement. As he was taking the frog, still in the cage, to his house, he thought about how he would prepare the frog.

The frog was really dirty from being in the creek pond, so he had to methodically wash the big frog to clean it up before he could cook it. The farmer decided not to remove the frog from the cage because he might get away. The cage was big and bulky, but it was just right to fit into the bathtub. The farmer decided to fill the bathtub with clean, fresh water and then put the cage holding the frog into the tub with the water. As the farmer lowered the frog and the cage into the tub of water, the frog became frantic and began jumping all around. The frog was really dirty, though, and the fresh, clean water was soon dirty and murky. The farmer drained the water, refilled the tub again, and, just as before, slowly lowered the frog and the cage into the tub of water. Again, the frog became frantic and began jumping all around inside the cage. Just as before, the frog was still quite dirty, and after a while, the water was dirty and murky all over again. The farmer drained the water and refilled it again, a third and fourth time, and just as before, each time, the frog became frantic and began jumping all around in the cage. Then, the farmer drained the tub but did not move the cage; he slowly filled the tub and cage with water. The frog and the cage were covered in the tub with water, and the frog did not begin frantically jumping all around in the cage.

The frog was beginning to enjoy itself and began swimming around in the tub within the cage. Just as before, the frog was still dirty, and after a while, the water was dirty and murky again. Each time, the frog enjoyed himself for longer periods before the farmer would have to drain and refill the tub with fresh, clean water. After the tenth time, the frog enjoyed itself in the water for a very long time, becoming **relaxed and comfortable.** The water was no longer dirty, and the frog was clean of the filthy creek pond water and ready to be cooked.

The farmer realized that he could not put the frog into the pot of hot water because it would immediately jump out. The farmer also knew the cage with the frog inside was too large to put into the pot. The farmer decided to refill the tub one more time with cool, clean water. The frog was really enjoying himself, so the farmer decided to wait till tomorrow to cook the frog. He left the frog comfortable in the cage with fresh, clean water for the rest of the evening and through the night.

Early the next day, around lunchtime, the farmer came to inspect the frog and found it resting calmly in the water, asleep with its head barely above the water. The farmer slowly removed some of the water from the tub, purposely not disturbing the frog. However, this time, the farmer was putting the water into the pot that he was going to use to cook the frog. The frog had become so comfortable around the farmer that the farmer could touch it and even pick it up in his hands. The farmer drained the tub one more time and removed the frog from the cage. This time, the farmer slowly lowered the frog into the water; this time, the farmer placed the frog in a pot of cool, comfortable, clean, and freshwater sitting on the stove.

As the farmer slowly lowered the frog into the pot of water sitting on the stove, it was as if the frog was really enjoying himself just as before. The farmer turned the heat very low to the pot on the stove; therefore, the pot heated up very, very, very slowly. Nonchalantly, the farmer returned to complete his daily tasks completely confident and convinced he would have frog stew for dinner. Around dinnertime, the farmer returned. Just as he had expected ...abracadabra... **cooked frog**. The farmer turned the frog over, and it appeared, by its peaceful facial expression, that the cooked frog had really been enjoying itself right down to the very end. Do not get caught up in satisfying yourself with the temporary comforts of life and imitation of *feel-good sensations*, or you might end up **a cooked**

frog. The young man knew to avoid life's comfort zones, but he himself, insidiously, had become a cooked frog. Now finding himself in active addiction, the young man can almost hear his grandmother saying, as she had said so many times throughout his life…" *Remember the cooked frog.*"

6

STOP THE MOVING TRAIN

Early in the morning, one day, while the young man was sitting in the park listening to a slow-moving train, just a stone's throw distance away, passing on the tracks located just behind a small thicket of tall pine trees, a Ferruginous Hawk flies' high overhead; a frolicking blue jay sings and plays on the branches of a maple tree growing mingled in front of several other rows of pine trees. Combined with the sounds of traffic, as each vehicle passes by on the outskirts of the park, the young man can hear the sounds of a distant train.

The distinct sounds and vibrations rising from the train suggest the train is slowing but is continuing to move. However, gradually and persistently, the train got slower and slower. The sounds of another train, an Amtrak passenger train, invade the sound waves and go swiftly by on one of the other sets of train tracks in the area. Turning to look toward his rear, the young man now notices another locomotive, a freight train, pacing down the tracks. This freight train is occupying one of the other four sets of train tracks, and this train is continuing to get noticeably slower.

The young man starts hearing shrieking and screeching, metal on metal, and grinding sounds of the train's engaging braking system. The gripping of the train's brake pads on the rolling wheels of this moving train is gradually slowing down this heavily loaded locomotive. The young man has consciously become more attuned and aware of this freight train, and as he **listens** more closely, the sounds from this freight train become more central. Nevertheless, in the distance, he hears another approaching engine, a fast-moving mass transit commuter train, as it swishes by on another of the four sets of tracks. **Listening,** becoming more conscious of present constructs of the young man's reality, and taking notice of present surrounding sights, sounds, singing birds, and blooming flowers and trees momentarily distract the young man's thoughts.

The raising of the young man's conscious awareness in the early morning daylight gave birth to an unforeseen and unintended beneficial consequence by diverting and refocusing the young man's mind away from mores of all-consuming, obsessive, and continuous thoughts of how he would get that first "hit" of the day, his thoughts in that present moment were disconnected, briefly disassociated from his cravings and compulsions.

The mental focus of the young man was momentarily not on the magnitude, the complexity, and incomprehensible hopelessness of the nature of his problems and dilemma. However, promptly, he was reminded of the undeniable and inescapable presence of a proverbial elephant in the living room. In the real and present inner belief and construct of the young man's reality, the undeniable and inescapable Goliath was obviously the predicament he had created for himself due to his addiction.

The young man had found himself a stowaway hostage on a high-jacked, out-of-control, and fully loaded high-speed freight train. He had purchased a ticket but boarded a camouflaged train heading to deceptive destinations he had no desire to visit. However, this train only offers one-way final destinations and no returns. Finding himself lost, he **recognizes and acknowledges** the certainty of his being out of control.

The young man admits he is unable **in and of himself** to actually stop the high-jacked speeding train. Furthermore, he is unable to avoid the inevitable **train wreck**. Therefore (he thinks), he will choose not to think about the truth of his deplorable situation because after he gets that hit, in pursuit of the *feel-good sensation* (high), everything will be better.

Immediately, upon completing that **thought and his inner self-talk,** the young man becomes even much more captivated and entranced, consciously aware of a sense of being in an apparently hypnotic state. Seemingly, he was being brought to that place or state of mind by the sounds coming from the loaded freight train. The locomotive is almost completely at a standstill, sluggishly moving but coming to a halt.

Conceivably, but incomprehensibly within himself, the young man was connecting the train's braking sounds with those he would cause as he was stopping his out-of-control train ride of active addiction and destructive behaviors. The sounds of the brake pads pressing against the metal wheels are becoming more and more pronounced in the background. The grinding and screeching sounds are alarming, frightful, shocking, disturbing, and startling. The disruptions (grinding) in life the young man will create as a result of stopping his train and unloading its freight are the unavoidable casualties of chemical dependency addiction and the destruction of addictive behaviors. This strange but prolific freight includes hurts and heartbreaks, weeping, crying, screaming, and the humiliation of disappointments. Not to forget the shattered feelings, the hateful expressions, the disgust, irreconcilable grievances, deep-rooted anger, unforgivable infractions, unsustainable and un-amenable relationships.

Such is life, neither fortunate nor unfortunate; it is what it is, just for now. As the young man exits from his train ride, he cannot express his deep and sincere regret. Therefore, his prayer for now is that someday he will receive forgiveness from those he harmed, fully aware and cognitive that some opportunities will have been lost, never to return. However, there are and will be many new opportunities, good memories, times of peace, serenity, happiness, tranquility, and some amenable relationships that can be salvaged.

The young man is consciously aware that the train in the background has come to a complete standstill. Now, fully aware that the train is at a complete standstill everything immediately seems quiet, and he feels an eerie but comforting peacefulness. Cognitively of the fact, as he **listened** closer to the sounds of the stopping train, he came to the point where he was not hearing anything else but the train. The fallout, distractions, and consequences of stopping the train to exit his *train wreck* of addiction will consume his full attention.

Furthermore, improving the circumstances of real-life reality will require a commitment of total effort of heart, might, mind, soul, and strength with all diligence and devotion. As such, entering the rehabilitation facility was fearful and frightening for the young man, and now he is feeling the shameful consequences of chemical dependency and active addiction, and the desire to escape the painful reality is excruciating. However, the pain, shame, and the "**humiliation of disappointment**" was more powerful than the fear.

Therefore, an abrupt stop to all communication from all outside sources (no phone calls, no letters, and no visits) was extremely therapeutic for the young man because it forced him to focus on himself. However, be forewarned, from the addict's warped and selfish perspective, this abrupt disconnect will be a hard pill to swallow. Albeit sometimes, it will prove to be even more difficult for non-addicted loving family members to support, to be in agreement, and to comply with. Even though communication through letters will usually be permitted in most in-house centers almost immediately upon admission, expect these letters to be read by the facility staff. On the other hand, usually, there can be no phone communication, and visitation is not permitted sometimes for up to as much as eight to ten weeks or longer, depending on circumstances.

The young man sincerely desired to see or talk to his wife, children, and other family members, but based on evidence-based trial and error and this young man's personal experiences, it has been proven, tried, tested, and found not to be in the best interest of the addicted individual in the early stage of the in-house residential recovery process.

Nevertheless, even if the addict had no direct contact with his family, knowing that family members thought enough to check up on them was uplifting and encouraging and helped to instill hope in the addict. Further humiliation of his total problem begins to come forcefully into focus within ten to fourteen days or so, with full details continuing to zoom into focus over the next 30 to 45 days. Therefore, for at least the first 90 days of real recovery, the recommendation for this young man is that he should not make any major decisions. Furthermore, some processes of recovery suggest that the individual should avoid, refrain from, and not start any new relationships for nearly eighteen months to two years. The focus for him, for the initial six months, should be on becoming educated about the holistic aspects and science of chemical dependency, addiction, and the recovery process.

All that being said, keep in mind that the desire, psychological craving, and the lure of powerful addictive tendencies are looking for excuses to leave the recovery center before completion of the program, and these tendencies are arrested.

For the non-addicted caring family members, you must be stronger and unwaveringly; you should never agree to the addict leaving any in-house residential facility prematurely or prior to completion of the structured program. Family members can support individuals through prayer and fasting to spiritually fight more effectively for loved ones. Remember: "This kind cometh out **except by prayer and fasting**" (Matt, 17:21). Non-addicted loved ones must surrender the addicted person to the care of the God of their understanding. Everyone had and "must need to" let everything related to the young man go and let God have HIS perfect way with him. This is the f.r.o.g.s. of life dilemma and the pathway to real addiction recovery. Of course, the young man felt unavoidable feelings of shame, worthlessness, desertion, humiliation, and frustrations in life that included feelings of real and perceived loneliness, hopelessness, helplessness, confusion, and abandonment.

7

THE FROG DILEMMA

Suddenly, during his time of extreme distress and anguish in rehab, it was as if the young man could see, in his mind's eye, a multiplicity of frogs. Also, he could hear his grandmother saying as she had said many times throughout his life... "Just remember the frogs." When life is filled with frustrations, rejections, obstacles, grievances, and sinful acts that seem to overwhelm you, "just remember the frogs."

Several times, the young man's grandmother had told him a part of the story from the bible about Moses and the frogs. During the time of the captivity of the Children of Israel to Pharaoh in Egypt, there were many plagues called down by God through Moses, the Prophet of the Lord, to persuade Pharaoh to let God's people, the Israelites, go. As recorded in the Bible, one of the plagues was the dilemma of frogs. The Bible indicates the abundant presence of frogs in Egypt was horrendous, overwhelming, and miraculously out of control. The frogs were literally coming from everywhere. Frogs were all through the houses, coming from all the lakes and rivers and all over the land. The frogs were all out of control; they were even in the ovens (see Ex. 8: 3). "This was truly a frog dilemma," the grandmother would say to the young man with a hint of the smirkiest smile on her face, that she would attempt to disguise. Interestingly enough, the lesson his grandmother wanted him to observe and surmise from the frog dilemma was related to when Pharaoh, and all of Egypt quite frankly, was fed up with the frogs. As the story goes, finally, Pharaoh sent for Moses and asked him to ask God to stop the frogs. Moses then immediately asked Pharaoh: When do you want the frogs to be gone?

The young man had been told the story more than two dozen times by his grandmother before she finally told him the lesson; she had always wanted him to ascertain and understand the frog dilemma and Pharaoh. Tears are swelling up in the eyes of the young man as he reflects on his grandmother's hesitation to explain the frog story.

The young man reflects upon his grandmother's final birthday party; with all her family gathered around her, his grandmother decided she would tell the rest of the frog story. It was at that moment that the young man realized that the grandmother had told the frog story to all of her children, grandchildren, and even to some of the kids in the neighborhood. However, she had not told the rest of the story to any of them. Everyone began to settle down in solemn reverence, silence, anticipation, and great expectation as she began to speak. Shortly after announcing, she had something she wanted to say to everyone.

As she began, she just repeated the story as she always had: The Bible indicates the abundant presence of the frogs in Egypt was horrendous, extremely frustrating, overwhelming, and miraculously out of control. The frogs were literally coming out from everywhere. Frogs were all through the houses, coming up from all the lakes and rivers, and all over the land was covered with frogs. The frogs were all out of control; they were even in the ovens and coming out of bed chambers. "This was truly a frog dilemma," the grandmother said to the young man as she became jovial and laughed out loud.

Then, the young man became aware that for all those years, his grandmother had announced for the first time she had been intrigued by the answer that Pharaoh had given to the question Moses had asked him. "Come closer, everyone," his grandmother softly voiced, almost in a whisper. "It was not the question," said the grandmother, "but it was the answer that Pharaoh gave: I want them gone tomorrow. The response from Pharaoh was diametrically interesting, and yet also a perplexing dichotomization, causing cognizant dissonance and confusion in my understanding of the frog dilemma, as it is recorded in the Bible" (see Exodus 8:9-10).

The grandmother, now sounding more like a college professor than the young man's little under-educated, elderly, and fragile grandma, continued, saying that for many years she had been really confused by Pharaoh's answer, that he wanted the frogs gone tomorrow. The young man's grandmother then revealed, to all the listening ears and the open hearts and minds of all those that were present, that when she was a child herself, her grandmother told her that same story. But she had always wondered if Pharaoh truly believed Moses could relieve, restore, free, and liberate Egypt from the frogs. If Pharaoh and all of Egypt were truly fed up with the frogs, why did Pharaoh not say he wanted the frogs gone "right now?" But instead, Pharaoh said tomorrow.

In other words, this grandmother explained to all those present that Pharaoh's answer was a way of saying, "Pharaoh wanted one more night with the frogs." Why would you ask for one more night of frogs in your bedroom, in your kitchen, in the bathroom, in the oven, and even in bed with you and your queen? The young man's grandmother, on her own birthday, had given all those present a gift of skillful and godly wisdom. She taught the frog story to the young man just as her grandmother had taught her, but that day, on her birthday, she taught the young man and all her family the rest of the frog story.

The young man now begins to recollect and remember that his grandmother also taught him to equate life's frustrations, rejections, negative attitudes, destructive behaviors, obstacles and oppositions, grievances, sinful acts, disagreements, and irreconcilable differences as frogs in your life. When our life choices produce frogs, don't stay confused in your thoughts of cognitive dissonance (the enemy of life is the author of confusion), and don't wait until tomorrow to ask God—Our Heavenly Father, The Creator, and Master Designer of all that exists, to remove the frogs and put them to death. Do it right now, today.

In the construct of the reality of his own choices, the young man finds himself caught in the train wreck of the frogs of addiction. In the midst of his crystal-clear reflection on his reality, the young man said it was as if he could hear his grandmother saying to him, "Get rid of the frog dilemma today; there is no need for you to wait till tomorrow." In the quiet moments of his days in recovery and rehabilitation facilities, it was as if the young man could hear his grandmother saying to him, just as she had said many times throughout his life... "Remember the dilemma of F.R.O.G.S."

8

FIVE FROGS ON A LOG

This gratefully recovering young man has been studying the Word of God since age (12), when he first considered the question: "Where did I come from? Why am I here, and where do I go after this life? Where did God come from? And who decided the color blue would be called blue instead of brown, black, purple, or orange?" He continually studies the Bible, sacred other Scriptures, and additional writings on Gospel topics by inspired leaders and teachers. A devotion to much study, meditation, pondering, fasting, and prayer has enlightened his mind and allowed this spiritual enlightenment to bless him with experiences, knowledge, understanding, skillful and godly practical wisdom on the art of living. Insights on vitally important daily concerns have to do with living life according to God's higher terms, based on divinely created destiny, rather than living life on primitive and lower terms of a strict physical existence and purpose.

Practical trial and error application of biblical principles, combined with years of reading, study, prayer, meditation, skillful godly wisdom, knowledge, and understanding gained from inspirational motivating books. Such exposures have given MrJames some choice experiences, preparatory to his presenting a unique perspective on chemical dependency and addiction, destructive addictive behaviors, and the recovery process. This young man now devotes his time, talents, and means to share his God-given insights for the purpose of raising awareness and magnifying successful Christ-centered recovery and how the application thereof can put to death the frogs of life.

Finding himself separated from God and feeling all alone, this young man's thoughts were turned to heaven, from whence came his *real help!* The road he traveled led him to recover from his separation from God due to chemical dependency and destructive addictive behaviors, which he labeled the road least traveled. However, his journey taught him rare, priceless, and valuable life lessons. The most fundamental truth of all that he emerged from the darkest abyss, helplessness, and uncontrollability of chemical dependency and addiction is:

"God is in control of all things."

This young man was well-liked and accepted by friends, classmates, teachers, neighbors, bosses, coworkers, and relatives. He served as freshman and sophomore class president during high school. He participated in many other academic and extracurricular activities. As a youth, he was a member of the Cub Scouts and Boy Scouts of America, where he attained the rank of Life Scout. He graduated in the top 20% of his high school graduating class.

The young man grew up in a small southern town in Alabama and had many friends and acquaintances. In particular, he had five brothers who were his closest neighborhood friends and with whom he grew up as a youth and adolescent. They were Bob Frog, Peter Frog, Earl Frog, Karl Frog, and Junior Frog. These friends lived life on the edge of excitement and to its full measure, always walking on the cusp of adventure, pushing themselves to experience the rush of the next *feel-good sensation.*

Consequently, in the process of time, each one of them became chemically dependent and **gradually** became active addicts of differing degrees of dependency by the time they finished high school. Individually, each of them, sooner or later, came to **accept** in the construct of their reality that each of them was addicted and they needed to change. It has been stated: "Permanent change is effective only when the need for change is understood, accepted, and internalized. In other words, that means that until the need or the incentive, cause, or reason to change is accepted inside as valuable and desired, the motivation to implement and execute changes in actions and behavior will be temporary and short-lived.

After graduating high school and taking a job promotion, the young man moved out of state and was immediately separated from all of his friends. Meeting together with his friends one last time before leaving town, they each made a decision and agreed they would stop using drugs. The young man left town and, for the next twelve years, only visited his hometown a sparse and limited number of times. Oftentimes, it is only for emergency family visits or other family matters. He never again saw all of his high school friends and brothers together again. Each of them, including himself, had continued to use mind-altering substances to satisfy that yearning within for the familiar experience of the *feel-good sensation.* In the process of time, the young man and each of his friends continued on their train ride, heading toward that final one-way destination and ending in a devastating train wreck.

Twenty years later, on an extended visit to his hometown, the young man picks up a newspaper and finds an alarming story on the front page of the local newspaper. The article listed the names of his high school acquaintances and friends. His brothers had been charged and were being indicted in a two-year undercover operation. Several others had been arrested and indicted for involvement in the transport of major drug trafficking and distribution between Florida and Texas.

One of his friends, Karl Frog, had reached that final one-way destination with no return; he died from an overdose from intravenous drug use. Another of the young man's friends was also caught up, actively addicted to intravenous drug use. Another of his friends had experienced a mental breakdown precipitated by illegal drug use. Another of his friends had enrolled in the military, where he served for 14 years. This friend's military career ended when he received a medical discharge due to conduct unbecoming as a direct result of alcoholism, chemical dependency, and addictive behaviors.

Junior Frog had also enlisted in the military, where he served for six years as he struggled with undiagnosed mental depression. He decided to end his military career prematurely to answer a call to serve his God as a missionary to Belgium. However, while struggling with depression, Junior Frog committed suicide on November 4, 2001.

Motivated by this tragic incident and the devastating train wrecks of his other friends' lives, this young man now shares his experiences to offer a sense of meaning and purpose to that horrific part of his life. The young man began to realize he was feeling shame, worthlessness, desertion, humiliation, frustration, loneliness, hopelessness, helplessness, abandonment, and confusion. While the young man was **reflecting** on those days, it was as if he could see in his mind's eye, the five frogs sitting on a log. In addition, the young man could hear his grandmother saying, as she had said many times throughout his life, *"Remember the frogs."*

Remembering that day and seeing in his mind's eye the five frogs sitting on a log in the middle of the farmer's pond, the young man hears his grandmother re-telling him the story about some frogs she had sent him to the pond to count. Said the grandmother to the young man, "There are five frogs sitting on a log in the middle of the pond. Three of the frogs have decided to jump off; will you go and see so you can tell me how many are left?" The grandson says there will be two frogs left, and the grandmother asks the young man, "Are you sure?" The grandson assures the grandmother that there will be two frogs left on the log, and he said he felt like he would be wasting his time walking all the way down to the pond to see **what he already knew**. The grandmother insists that her grandson goes to see the frogs on the log.

When he arrives at the pond, **nothing has changed**; he notices there are still five frogs on the log. He returns home and tells his grandmother what he saw. The grandmother, unresponsive and showing no expression, after a passing while, again says to the grandson, "There were five frogs sitting on a log in the middle of the pond, but *four* of the frogs have now decided to jump off; will you go back and see, and **let me know** how many frogs are left now?" The grandson said, "Grandmother, there will be one frog left."

The grandmother asks her grandson, "Are you sure?" The grandson assures the grandmother that there will be one frog left. Just as before, the young man felt he would be wasting his time walking all the way down to the pond to see what he **already knew**. Knowing that his grandmother would insist that he go to see how many frogs were left sitting on the log, away, he went.

When the grandson arrives at the pond this time, again, nothing has changed; he notices there are still five frogs on the log. Again, he returns home and tells his grandmother what he saw. The grandmother is quite unresponsive for a longer while this time, but again, she says to her grandson, "There were five frogs sitting on a log in the middle of the pond. However, all *five frogs* have now decided to jump off the log; will you go and see and **let me know** if there are any frogs left sitting on the log now?"

The grandson said, "If all five frogs decide to jump off the log, there will not be any frogs left sitting on the log in the pond."

The grandmother again quietly asks her grandson, "Are you sure? The grandson, for the third time, assures his grandmother that there will not be any frogs left sitting on the log in the pond, and this time, the young man really feels he would be wasting his time walking all the way down to the pond for the third time. Just to see what he **already knew**. However, knowing that his grandmother would insist that he go to see how many frogs would be left sitting on the log, albeit reluctantly, he hurried off to the pond.

When he arrives at the pond, **nothing has changed;** he notices that there are still five frogs sitting on the log. He returns home irritated and somewhat disgusted. With an apparent attitude, the young man informs his grandmother in this manner, "Three, four, maybe even all five of those frogs may have decided to jump off the log, but they are all still sitting there very dry and haven't done anything yet."

Then, rather excited and animated, the grandmother told the grandson that he was exactly right. "My dear son, those frogs had only made a decision to jump, but they never did anything about that decision; they did not do anything different at all. Thus, you can see deciding to make a change is only part of the process leading to real change. Remember, my son, 'If nothing changes, nothing will change.'"

Those five frogs acting on a decision to change would facilitate the frogs having to get wet. There was no way the frogs could remain dry if they acted upon their decision to jump off the log. Similarly, after making the decision to learn to ride a bicycle, there is possibly no way to act upon that decision and not fall down a few times. When the fullness of the time to change arrives, the time to prepare to make the change has already passed. Acting on decisions to change will facilitate the proverbial *getting wet syndrome.* Conversely, a decision to begin the process of recovery from addiction and addictive behaviors requires making a decision to change and requires a firm **commitment** to endure the consequences of that decision. Go ahead, decide to change, **jump in, and get wet,** but just do it now.

Reflecting on the loss of Junior Frog, the grandson saw in his mind's eye the five frogs sitting on a log in the pond. He could also hear his grandmother saying, just as she had said many times throughout his life... "Remember the five frogs."

9

THE PROCESS OF CHANGE

The longer this young man lives, and the more knowledgeable he becomes, the more his understanding of the natural or physical world confirms there is an eternal law or principle known as "The Law of Cause and Effect." This knowledge helps increase his understanding of spiritual reality. Life, in its simplest state, consists of yesterday, today, and tomorrow. However, the most important component in the process of life is today, and science, nature, and personal experience confirm that nothing really remains the same. All things either act or are acted upon, constantly moving either positively or negatively, progressing forward or moving backward, and nothing just stands still and remains in that state of being. Therefore, standing still and not doing anything to move forward is equal to moving backward if everything else is moving forward ever so slowly. At the beginning of time, when all was void, and darkness was on the face of the deep…God said, "Let there be light." Since then, change has and will continue to occur without ceasing; thus, change is inevitable and is set in motion, sustained, and controlled by laws of cause and effect.

Therefore, ponder the question: *What happened to darkness? Did it disappear? Evaporate?* This young man believes it did neither disappear nor evaporate. This young man is referencing another eternal law known as: *"The Law of Displacement,"* first introduced in Genesis Chapter 1, when God said, *"Let there be light."* God saw darkness but said what he wanted; HE did not speak what HE saw. He called things that are not as though they were (Rom 4:17; Mosiah 16: 6), and in doing so, He established this as a governing eternal principle for our benefit in earthly existence. The principle is that *darkness must give way to Light.* Darkness was there, but Light was placed as preeminent and supreme. When God said, "Let Light be," Darkness could continue to exist, but not in the same place at the same time as Light. As Light enters, Darkness is removed from its place. Thus, we have what this young man calls: *"the law of Displacement."*

This young man suggests getting up early one morning, just before the sun comes up. Go off to an area where you can see off in a distance in an eastward direction. A wide-open field area or a view up the mountainside would be perfect. Watch in the easterly direction as the sun begins to rise and darkness begins to move. You are looking to see what happens when the light of the sun rising out of the east meets the darkness. If your point of view on this phenomenon is sufficient, you will see the law of displacement in its purest form, as it was first introduced by God—Our Heavenly Father, The Creator, and Master Designer of all that exists. When this young man witnessed this for himself, it appeared as if the darkness was literally, and in reality, running from the light as it illuminated the areas covered by darkness.

Consequently, this young man purports that the most efficient, the most productive, and the most profitable, and beneficial use of our energy and effort is to understand the causes that will produce the change we desire that will make our lives better. It does not matter whether we are trying to change our minds, our will, or our emotions. Even if we are trying to change personality, attitude, or behaviors, the eternal principles will always be the same. Therefore, this young man suggests identifying the desired change and applying the proper process that will bring the desired effect, and because of the *"law of cause and effect"* and *"the law of displacement,"* you will, in due time, produce the expected change in the manifest construct of your new reality.

However, the process that will produce a change for the better is not without struggle. The secret, however, is to apply the methods proven not to fail, then *"let"* the process work to bring about your expected results. With reference to the changing of behavior, this young man realizes that permanent changes in behavior must start with an internal change in our hearts or in our minds. This young man believes any man convinced against his will is of the same opinion.

CHANGE TODAY, NOT NOW, BUT RIGHT NOW!

Remember this: Change does not change until some...thing changes.

Therefore, this young man believes this can only begin in our intellect. Our intellect is made up partly of the information we allow to enter into our brain: what we read, what we see with our eyes, what we hear through our ears, etc., even the pains and aches of our body. Any efforts to change behavior that does not take into account a change in our intellect will be ineffective and short-lived (Rom 12:1-2). Continuing to do the same things over and over but expecting different results describes insanity. Let us all realize, understand, and accept that *"change is not change until some... thing changes."*

We must choose to...Submit Ourselves to the Process of Change and then,

LET CHANGE HAPPEN!

Submitting to *the process of change* is a major step in becoming what we were created to become and transforms human beings into "humans becoming." Sometimes, this young man feels like waiting on God, our Heavenly Father, to move on our behalf is a punishment in itself. However, in reality, he knows waiting on God can never be a punishment in reality. But, wait on the miracle, having no idea of how it will happen or what will or will not happen. Furthermore, I do not know when it will happen. This young man reminds us to be comforted and even become increasingly more comfortable knowing that Heavenly Father's timing is always perfect. Learning to wait on God is a necessary experience for us all.

Adam and Eve had to wait outside of the Garden of Eden. Adam was at the ripe old age of 939 when he died. Noah and his family waited on the Ark, with the animals, dung, urine, and all, for one year and ten days, according to today's calendar, for the "process of change" to complete the full cycle. Additionally, the children of Israel had to spend 40 years wandering in the wilderness; Sarah and Abraham also waited for the birth of the promised child, and they were nearly 100 years old. Conversely, the Three Hebrew boys waited on God even though they were thrown into the fiery furnace. Daniel waited on God but was thrown into the lions' den; Lehi and Sariah waited on God to send their sons back from the Palace of Laban; the Prophet Enos waited on God in prayer, all day, all night, and all day again; Ammon waited on God, serving a king that thought Ammon was his enemy. This young man remembers it was the brother of Jared who waited on God, and he saw the Finger of God move on his behalf. Likewise, the Prophet Jonah waited three days in the belly of that big fish, just as the Body of Christ waited in the tomb till the third day, and it was then that the miracle of the Resurrection became a reality.

This young man thanks God for the Spirit that brings these things to memory. Waiting on God in righteousness and doing what is right is all we can do.

"THE MAIN THING IS TO KEEP THE MAIN THING, THE MAIN THING."

This young man has learned from personal experiences that blessings come because we are obedient to the eternal laws that bring the associated blessings into our lives. There is no other way to manifest permanent change and transformation except as a result of waiting on God's perfect timing.

CLOSING THOUGHT:

HELLO, THIS IS GOD. I WILL BE HANDLING ALL OF YOUR PROBLEMS

TODAY. I WILL NOT NEED YOUR HELP. THANK YOU. HAVE A NICE DAY.

(Author unknown)

"Let THE PROCESS OF CHANGE transform you and your loved one."

10

A MESSAGE TO: THE FAMILIES OF ADDICTS

Wisdom from the young man...

This young man is saying to you, family members, and the addict: "Do not be led to believe in false hopes; believe in **nothing, absolutely nothing** other than "the" power that is greater than ourselves; that power is God." "The" power may be called by other names: Jesus, the Lord, Jehovah, Heavenly Father, Supreme Being, Creator, Most High God, The Almighty, and other labels such as these. This young man is saying to you, caring family members, in no uncertain terms, that the foundation for recovery must be spiritual in nature and essence.

Moreover, this young man wants to be crystal clear on this point: any sense of confidence in anything other than *"All-Powerful"* is formal denial, and D.E.N.I.A.L is the enemy of real recovery. Therefore, this young man recognizes his personal experiences have confirmed for him that a **powerful, cunning,**

baffling, and *relentless* symptom of chemical dependency, addiction, relapse, and addictive behaviors.

All you mothers, fathers, husbands, wives, sons, brothers, sisters, daughters, relatives, and other concerned persons, the message from this young man to you is that life in a drug rehabilitation center can be pure **hell on earth**. But he thanks God daily for them. Conversely, living life in bondage to chemical dependency, addiction, relapse, and addictive behaviors is more excruciating than someone wandering around with inner excruciating pain, waiting and sometimes hoping to topple over and die so as to be pushed into a grave, covered over, and put out of misery.

When a family member is making the choice and is insistent and persistent about a loved one entering, participating, and completing a rehab program, making the choice may be embarrassing for the family. However, it is a decision void of D.E.N.I.A.L. and is a decision that is in the best interest of the addicted individual. Barring none, this young man is grateful to all those who had the strength of character, in the pressure of the moment, to support his decision to admit himself to rehab.

All that being said, it is overwhelmingly tough for many family members not to hate the addict, hate their addictive behaviors, and even hate the person who has become a slave of addiction. As used and recognized by this young man, hate— the strongest **negative** emotion in all of eternity—is the diametric opposite of love. Moreover, love is the strongest and the most **positive** emotion in all of eternity. This young man has learned from his personal experiences that both words should be used with caution, particularly in the world of chemical dependency, relapse, addiction, and addictive behaviors.

Keep in mind that there are inherent and unintended consequences in the wake associated with the use of both words. This young man—a brother, an uncle, a husband, a father, a dad, a grandfather, and a child of God—also believes pure, unselfish **LOVE** is stronger than chemical dependency, addiction, relapse, and addictive behaviors. The love of family must be tough, strong, and potent as an unfailing remedy for chemical dependency, relapse, and addiction and to arrest addictive behaviors. Moreover, the love of God that flows through the testimony of Jesus Christ is perfect; it restores hope and faith in the belief that chemical dependency, relapse, addiction, and destructive addictive behaviors can be put to death.

11

TOUGHER TO LOVE, HATE COMES TOO EASY

Yes, tougher **love** is precisely what it would take, and tougher love was exactly what this young man needed to force him to turn inward toward his genuine inner self. The real person—the grandson, the husband, the father, the brother, the spiritual child of God of yesteryears—was to be resurrected, called forth from under the constriction of chemical dependency, relapse, addiction, and addictive behaviors.

This young man had promised his wife the world; he was the father of her children, as only he could—he had shown unfailing love for his family for more than two decades. This was that same person who was loved and respected by sisters, brothers, aunts and uncles, in-laws, and neighbors. Moreover, this exact same person had served in church and civic leadership positions. This person absolutely could not be that same person now acting out destructive, disappointing, humiliating, insane, inexcusable, and unexplainable behaviors.

The weight of the associated feelings, the *humiliation of the disappointment,* the shame, the embarrassment, the pain, and the heartfelt hurt the young man was causing his family coalesced, combining together to become synergistically a more powerful emotion than anything this young man had ever felt or experienced. However, the bitter tang and the dichotomy in the construct of his reality, it was his own actions that were destroying his family—the very thing in life that had given his life worthwhile purpose, meaning, and real substance. Furthermore, the young man was not in control of his life, and his life truly was hopelessly unmanageable. This young man described this phase of active addiction as *"crazed insanity."* Additionally, further purports that his actions, deeds, and behavior were unreasonable and utterly foolish.

There is **nothing, absolutely nothing,** that the young man can do about actions, deeds, and addictive behaviors from the past, nor can anything be done to erase them. Just for today, he acknowledges it is what it is, for right now. Today, he is thankful and grateful to have further enlightenment, knowledge, and understanding of chemical dependency, addiction, relapse, and addictive behaviors. His unwavering hope is that one day, he will be forgiven by those he scared and injured, realizing he must also come to willingly forgive himself, which is a major component in the success of any recovery program.

Exactly what is this proverbial *"tough love,"* and how is it properly implemented and dispersed? This young man asks the question because he may have witnessed both proper and improper actions claiming to be disbursed under the auspices of tough love. This young man, more than once, has experienced intentional ill-treatment at the hands of others simply because of his status as an "addict." Therefore, when taking your actions, you are labeled under the umbrella of "tough love." this young man cautions family members and others: Be genuine, authentic, without vengeance, and without malicious intent levied toward the addict; you be the judge.

It is noted, from this young man's personal experience, that inflicting punishing acts and punitive type actions improperly administered and implemented as "tough love" can be confusing and devastating to an addict, and the unintended consequence can even be fatal. Therefore, this young man must admit his initial understanding of "tough love" changed completely and transformed to be described as *"tougher love."* Traditional characteristics of tough love that were reflected toward the addict wreaked havoc and would usually connote family disassociation, isolation, and eventually complete family separation.

According to this young man, it is not unusual for the addict to be put out on the street, such that a major percentage of active addicts inevitably become homeless and become fugitives and vagabonds, living from place to place. Family members, under the auspices of "tough love," and oftentimes motivated with pure motives, throw out clothes, take keys, lock doors, change locks, call the police, physically assault, and verbally attack them. This young man has witnessed a diverse number of other disparaging actions as well, usually described as acts of "tough love" and meant to communicate to the addict:

"...get out of my life! I don't want anything to do with you!"

For this young man, it was his wife saying the familiar words and taking similar actions. In the construct of the reality of the addicted, the addict's sense of meaning in life could be connected to them.

Keeping all the aforementioned things in mind, this young man also reminds family members that the inner conflict, the confusion, the *humiliation of disappointment,* and the pursuit of the artificially produced, counterfeit *feel-good sensation* produce insanity in the addict's behavior. Accordingly, based on the experiences of this young man, this insanity is manifesting itself in constantly shifting values, irresponsibility, and **lying and stealing;** this stage of dependency is uncontrollable by the addict without intervention, rehabilitation, or a structured source of treatment. These actions are indeed aspects of the nature of chemical dependency, addiction, relapse, and destructive addictive behavior patterns.

Furthermore, without a proper source of structured treatment, the symptoms can be arrested temporarily, experiencing frequent relapses but not permanently being controlled. However, the young man thinks, comparatively speaking, this is similar to the symptoms of diabetes, high blood pressure, cancer, or any other deviation of the body from its normal healthy state, which must also be controlled. This young man came to realize that chemical dependency, addiction, relapse, and destructive addictive behavior patterns could not be relieved without proper diagnosis and a type of structured treatment environment and program.

12

CRYSTAL CLEAR

This young man:

"I must make myself completely understood;
Crystal clear, pristine, and not misunderstood on this issue."

This young man is not saying...families should allow addicts to misuse and abuse them. He is not even suggesting that loved ones allow their personal property to be stolen, sold, pawned, or destroyed. Conversely, he is not saying to furnish addicts with the means and opportunity to buy or use drugs.

"I wish you were dead. Just leave, and I never want to see you again." These words continue to ring in this young man's ears. His wife shouted those words at him, the last time he acted out in his destructive addictive behavior, before going into the final rehab. This young man had taken money his wife had set aside to buy her a car. She said, **"I will never forgive you for this. Why are you doing this to us?"** His wife was never able to forgive him completely. However, today, the young man is clean, serene, and redeemed.

An addict caught in the grips of their addiction has no

answer to questions such as these: **Why are you doing this to us?** If this young man had known the answer to that question, he may have walked the pathway of recovery much sooner and avoided many of the pitfalls of addiction, relapse, and recovery.

Furthermore, the thoughts and feelings associated with the truthful answers to these questions and the onset of **"humiliation of disappointment"** associated with the answer are much too painful. Therefore, such questions and the related pain connected to the answers serve only to send him, the active addict, deeper into using--off to the races in pursuit of the *feel-good sensation*. The love of the young man's family was vital and crucial, the most important link in the chain, providing him a means of escaping the grips of chemical dependency, addiction, relapse, and destructive addictive behavior patterns.

With that being said, this young man has heard many suggestions from various individuals indicating that loving family members must put the addict out of their lives. To this addicted young man, active in my addiction, that would have been like throwing him, a drowning man, a rock instead of a rope. The only sanity, stability, and real serenity in the young man's life, during the peak of his chemical dependency and addiction, periods of relapse, and when he would act out addictive behaviors, was his family. Nevertheless, the young man's thoughts of his wife and children and his helplessness over his chemical dependency and destructive actions endlessly tormented him.

The young man's family relationships, even though put under tremendous stress, are what prevented him from giving up altogether, giving in to the all-consuming nature of his cravings, giving in to absolute chemical dependency, and the *"crazed insanity"* of his destructive, addictive behaviors. The young man's family connection and love of God served as a lifeline and buoy, keeping him afloat, not succumbing to the enticement to become a fugitive and a vagabond on the life plain. This young man became very acquainted with many such individuals who had given up on their life journey. For these individuals, their journey through addiction, recovery, and relapse transformed them into that very thing: fugitives and vagabonds.

The small **flicker of hope** he held onto was rooted in a belief, without any doubt, that he had family members who loved him. However, the young man's destructive thoughts and initial **negative self-talk** always tried to convince him otherwise. For more than two decades, he and his family had been relationship-building as they engaged in the art of living within the confines of a loving family. As such, the young man carried with him, through addiction and recovery, remnant knowledge of assurance of each other's love. He is expressly thankful to his wife because, at the peak of dependency, he refused to accept any belief that his wife would totally turn away from him.

Nonetheless, some of the things the young man did and his selfish and seemingly uncaring actions suggested to his wife and all others who cared that they should get as far away from him as possible. Thus, one could see that when an addict was not under the influence of the pull of compulsive cravings, the addict was under the influence of guilt, shame, and ***humiliation of disappointment***. The active addict engages in accusatory condemning self-talk, such that the addicts can no longer stand looking at themselves in the mirror.

However, in the quiet confines behind their eye, between the ears, and within themselves, as the saying goes: ***"To thy own self be true."*** As an addict, this young man really needed the unconditional love of another human being. Additionally, he needed to be reminded of the pure love of God, Our Heavenly Father, for the addict, and he needed a deeper understanding of the gift of the *at-one-ment* of Jesus Christ. Furthermore, the addict needs to accept the **at-one-ment** of Jesus Christ as the foundation upon which the addict should begin building or rebuilding a closer, more intimate relationship with God. The addict needed to know of the surety of God's forgiveness of the addict's sins of addiction.

Consequently, the young man testifies that if the addict is left alone in the physical, conscious, material world of the addict, it will be difficult for the addict to focus on, concentrate on, and penetrate the realm of the love of God. Furthermore, as testified to by the young man, the addict being left alone becomes an open target of the cravings and obsessions of the lures and enticements of addictive behavior. Therefore, *remember* that an active addict left alone is always in bad company. *The enemy is the inner me.*

13

REMEMBER THE FROG

Nov 4th, 2001

Darrell James Campbell, Jr. (26) years old, committed suicide, suffering from depression. Most (addicts) alcoholics and many family members deny the existence of addiction, sometimes unto death. However, this young man believes the most important of all the things he has to say would be focused on the crippling, debilitating, cunning, and baffling maggot of "DENIAL," associated with addiction, and is the primary enemy of recovery.

This blessed and highly favored young man is grateful to be one of those who are in the process of recovering from a drug addiction that almost cost him everything: his wife, trust, family, self-respect, sentimental material possessions, and almost his very life. The violent, addictive behavior of an alcoholic stepfather resulted in the death of the young man's birth mother.

This young man urges you, the reader, to understand that I believe the most detrimental, destructive symptom of addiction is the D.E.N.I.A.L of its existence. Specifically, this young man is highlighting the D.E.N.I.A.L. of the addicted person, the D.E.N.I.A.L. of the non-addicted family members, and the D.E.N.I.A.L. of co-dependents and enablers. Sometimes, these are friends, sometimes relatives, sometimes casual acquaintances, and sometimes even parents. D.E.N.I.A.L is a contributing factor in many of the fatalities resulting directly and indirectly from chemical dependency, addiction, and destructive addictive behaviors. D.E.N.I.A.L. is a cunning, deceptive, and powerful facilitator of addictions and equally one of the most destructive symptoms of chemical dependency and all other addictions. To be perfectly clear, this young man truly believes that when it is understood appropriately, D.E.N.I.A.L will be recognized as an inseparable component in the progression of the stages of addiction.

Moreover, may this young man be crystal clear in asserting his belief, seeing D.E.N.I.A.L. as a pervasive unintended consequence of chemical dependency and other addictions? Consequently, this young man believes much of the heartache, some of the pain of relapse, and some of the "humiliation of disappointments" can be minimized by embracing the process of becoming more knowledgeable about the evidenced-based addiction recovery processes.

The personal experience of this young man in his battle against chemical dependency and addiction, D.E.N.I.A.L., was the symptom preventing him from recovering. This knowledge about D.E.N.I.A.L., when received, accepted, and internalized, can potentially make quite a difference.

The significant others in the life of the addicted person, even seeing sufficient evidence, will deny the existence of an addiction. Such that the continual refusal to accept and acknowledge the truth, D.E.N.I.A.L. allows all the dimensions of the budding addict—mental, social, physical, spiritual, psychological, spiritual, and physiological—to become contaminated. The destruction of logical reasoning and mental capacity negatively serves the D.E.N.I.A.L. aspect of chemical dependency, depending on the reaction from the non-addicted. The mental contamination of chemical dependency thrives on the D.E.N.I.A.L. of its existence, allowing the worsening of effects as the addiction continues to progress to later stages.

This brings this young man to another point that needs to be understood by the caring loved ones and the addicted. Deal with the D.E.N.I.A.L. first!

"If you don't know where you are going, any road takes you there.

Before you know how to get there, you must first know
Where you want to go. Then, you must know
Where you are now."

14

THOUGHTS, WORDS, TERMS

Before concluding, here are my definitions and understanding of some terms that will be used going forward in the process of recovery and putting *death to frogs*. I put this list forward to minimize potential misunderstandings so that we may better understand one another.

SYMPTOM - A specific abnormal behavior is referred to as **a symptom.**

ABNORMAL BEHAVIOR -The definition of **abnormal behavior** may depend on the culture and on social values. Persons with an impaired ability to meet daily responsibilities, however, are likely to be regarded in most societies as exhibiting abnormal behavior (Compton's Ency. 1999, Mental Illness).

SYNDROME - Several symptoms usually found in combination are collectively referred to as **a syndrome.**

DENIAL -The absolute refusal to accept facts, physical evidence, feelings, or intuitions as sufficient indications of the possible presence of a chemical dependency in "your loved one."

DENIAL SPEAKS - This is **the voice of DENIAL** addiction, DUI, jail, losing jobs, and loved ones going into rehab. It happens in other families, but not ours. This happened to my husband's family (my wife's family), but there is no way my child is an addict. I can stop anytime I want to. I cannot believe you did that; I will never do that again.

INTRODUCTION TO AN ADDICT – there is a pattern of abnormal behavior and reactions: lies about money being lost or stolen and constantly makes excuses for otherwise unexplainable behavior. Remember, an addict lies "whenever he/she opens his/her mouth," and *every* addict will lie, manipulate, steal, and cheat. The progressive effects of addiction infecting the individual and family are based on dishonesty and denial. Therefore, expect no honesty from an active addict. If the story sounds bizarre or unbelievable, do not believe it. This young man insists that the sooner you adopt this basic philosophy when interacting with the addict, the better. An addict can hide their hands for a while, some longer than others, but they will never have anything to show for the missing money; bills and financial obligations will be neglected. An addict's unaccountable money will always tell the rest of the story, and the money will have been stolen or lost, or they will have been cheated or robbed. Immediately, you should become discontented and alarmed. This should especially be true of your reactions if there is a similar second incident. Once it is suspected that drug use, drug abuse, chemical dependency, addiction, relapse, or addictive cravings could be the cause of some abnormal behavior, the benefit of the doubt should not ever be given to the suspected addict. If you are wrong, quickly admit it, but confrontation could be the pathway to save an addict's life. As an active addict, this young man said he never deserved the proverbial "benefit of the doubt."

PSYCHOLOGISTS ARE SAYING... an area of the brain affected by mind-altering chemicals, illegal drugs, prescription drugs, street drugs, narcotics, and habitual destructive addictive behavior patterns is the prefrontal cortex (UCLA, 2000). This is where logical, rational, and executive thinking takes place in the brain. If this is true, and for the sake of this man's argument, take the position that it is true. Bearing that truth in mind, don't think you are ever going to talk an addict into the choice of starting the recovery process. This young man argues that *a man convinced against his will is of the same opinion*. Additionally, from the perspective of this being true about the way an active addict thinks, how can a sober-minded person ever expect an abandoned, addicted person, permanently left alone, to recover all by themselves? The addicted person's perceptions of issues, facts, details, and memories of incidents are distorted. If it is true that mind-altering drugs adversely affect the areas in the brain responsible for regulating logical and rational thinking, therefore, active in addiction, the addicted person's thinking becomes contaminated, mind-altered, and "hijacked" (www.health.harvard.edu). Narcotics are mind-altering drugs that can actually change the body chemistry in such a way that normal functioning becomes impossible unless the drug is present (Compton's Encyc. 1999 Addiction & Withdrawal). Consequently, becoming acquainted with several homeless individuals and families, this young man soon came to ascertain many of his new acquaintances had been ushered into the roadway of homelessness due to abandonment, aloneness, isolation, and sometimes rebellion. On the other hand, sometimes, individuals were fleeing physical, mental, verbal, or sexual abuse. Nonetheless, for many individuals, what was once considered abnormal behavior became a major component in the new normal construct of their reality.

What this means is that any thought you may have of talking an addicted person out of their schizophrenic, unrealistic reality without an internal change of heart is a thought rooted and grounded in *ignorance* about the science and principles of addiction, and if blatant evidence that you are caught in the "denial syndrome." Any person addicted to mind-altering substances for extended periods truly thinks differently. You can talk to this person until both of you are blue in the face, but the odds are stacked overwhelmingly against you, talking them into recovery. This is one of the reasons only 8-10% of those entering traditional 12-step programs remain drug-free. Continuing in active addiction, according to Dr. Janice Phelps, "does not result primarily from emotional stress, a lack of willpower or other psychological factors" (Phelps, MD. 1986). For this young man, he had to first **decide** and then **internalize** that he was addicted.

TOUGH LOVE... *you better believe it!* This young man is thankful to his family that today he is found in that greater than 50% group celebrating his recovery. He is thankful to God for the authentic family love they all had for each other, especially the spoken words, filled with faith, by his son. When all hope seemed lost for the young man, this son said, "Mother, I am going to believe Dad will overcome this." It is tougher to love an addict in spite of themselves or at least their addicted self. Today, this young man's life has hope, and he is so thankful that in spite of all his addictions carried their family through, there was always at least one other human being believing absolutely that he was a soul worth.

The fasciculus *retroflexus—*

NICOTINE CAUSES SELECTIVE DEGENERATION IN BRAIN, UCLA NEUROSCIENTISTS REPORT

ScienceDaily (Nov. 10, 2000) — Nicotine causes degeneration in a region of the brain that affects emotional control, sexual arousal, REM sleep, and seizures, UCLA neuroscientists report in the current issue of the journal Neuropharmacology. "Nicotine causes the most selective degeneration in the brain that I have ever seen," said UCLA neuroscientist Gaylord Ellison, a professor of psychology and member of UCLA's Brain Research Institute. "Only one tract of the brain is affected." The part of the brain that is affected by nicotine is called fasciculus retroflexus, which has two halves.

In previous research conducted over more than two decades, Ellison's research team has shown that such drugs as amphetamines, cocaine, and ecstasy damage one-half of fasciculus retroflexus. In the journal Neuropharmacology (Society for Neuroscience), Ellison's research team reports for the first time that nicotine causes degeneration in the other half of fasciculus retroflexus. The neuroscientists further report that the drugs that damage one-half of fasciculus retroflexus do not damage the other half that nicotine affects. **"Our findings suggest that this (fasciculus retroflexus) is the brain's weak link for stimulant addictive drugs,"** Ellison said. "This tract is affected more by chronic drug use than any other tract in the brain... **"It seems likely that fasciculus retroflexus is linked to drug addiction and relapse,"** Ellison said. "In chronic smokers, this tract may well play a major role in the addiction to nicotine." The Fasciculus retroflexus **pathway is a part of the brain that is not well understood.**

Ellison has studied the effects of drugs on the brain for

more than 20 years. His research is funded by the National Institute of Drug Abuse and the Tobacco-Related Disease Research Program, which is funded by California's tobacco tax.

University Of California, Los Angeles (2000, November 10). Nicotine Causes Selective Degeneration in Brain, UCLA Neuroscientists Report. *ScienceDaily*. Retrieved April 6, 2012, from http://www.sciencedaily.com **/releases/2000/11/001110073314.htm**
Bottom of Form

15

PRAYER AND FASTING

FAST REFLECTION: LAW OF FAST

Fasting has been observed and practiced since the days of Moses, and evidence of observance continued throughout the Old Testament, up to and including the prophet Zachariah in 520-518 B.C. (Exodus 34:28; Zac 7:3-7, 8:18-19). Furthermore, Jesus observed the fast for forty days and forty nights (Matt 4:2). Additionally, Jesus taught the significance of his disciples utilizing fasting for the purpose of casting out some persistent, more difficult demons (Mark 9:14-29).

Inarguably, there is considerable evidence recorded in the four Gospels of the ritualistic practice of fasting prior to and during the time of Christ (Luke 2:36-37; 5:33). Moreover, observance of fasting after the time of Jesus' ascension is equally documented in the New Testament record as well (Acts 10:30,13:1-3,14:23; 1 Cor 6:5, 11:27).

Nevertheless, fasting had become wholly perverted as it was practiced by the children of Israel during the time of Isaiah, and likewise perverted as practiced by Scribes, Pharisees, and hypocrites during the time of Christ (Isa 58:3-5; Mall 6:16).

However, when Jesus was questioned by the disciples of John Baptist and the Pharisees, highlighting or emphasizing their ritualistic practice of fasting, and the non-observance of fasting practiced by the disciples of Jesus, He affirmed the practice and doctrine of fasting but dismissed the need for the disciples of Jesus too fast as long as He, Jesus, the Bridegroom was with them (Luke 5:33-35; Matthew 9:14-15).

Additionally, Jesus was questioned by murmuring Scribes about his followers' lack of fasting. Even so, it is the second part of His answer, which He gives to the crowd in His customary form of parables in blind eyes and to deaf ears that this young man will now refer to. The symbolic metaphor of old and new wine and wineskins, and the old cloth and new patches on garments that Christ utilized in this parable, this young man finds to be quite revealing (Luke 5:36-38; Matt 9:16-17). As I have pondered this parabolic answer given by Jesus, it has piqued my interest, elevated my cognitive dissonance, thereby producing more questions, and has increased my consciousness to an awareness of some unique Latter-day significance of fasting.

Consequently, this young man's reflection has given birth to two specific questions within his inner being. First: Is the old practice of fasting in its perverted forms to be done away with? And, second: Does this newborn spiritual creation require the re-instituted, non-perverted practice and private observance of fasting as described in Isaiah 58:6? This young man believes it could be argued that the answer to both questions should be an emphatic yes!

Moreover, biblical evidence seems to suggest, without much dispute, that fasting had been practiced and observed anciently; however, during the time of Isaiah, 740-701 B.C., the laws, concepts, principles, and practice of fasting had become wholly perverted. This perversion continued through the times of Zachariah in 520-518 B.C., as recorded by this prophet in one of the final writings of the Prophets of the Old Testament.

Nevertheless, is it coincidental, incidental, or an intentional prerequisite that Jesus begins His ministry on the foundation of an extended observance of fasting? Furthermore, this young man is reminded that the perverted forms of fasting were denounced by Jesus (Mall 6:16-18), but fasting was affirmed by Him as a needed and necessary practice for His disciples to observe (Mark 9:29); after Jesus the Bridegroom is no longer with them (Mall 9:15). More specifically, Jesus taught that there was a need for new vessels (body, temple, bottles) and new garments (wineskins, cloths, thoughts, and beliefs) to accommodate, preserve, and maintain the new creation conceived at the birth of born-again Christians (Luke 2:21-22).

Therefore, the perverted form of fasting (old garment) and the worldly practice of fasting (old wineskins, old bottle) must be disbursed, discarded, and replaced with observance of the true order and law of fasting as the Lord had instructed his children to observe through the prophet Isaiah in 740-701 B.C. This young man is deeply cognizant of the total and complete details the Lord espouses when he explains the purpose, the process, and the attendant and corresponding blessings associated with fasting. Conversely, through the Prophet Isaiah, the Lord denounced the perversion of fasting using no uncertain terms and, in conclusion, saying, "Thus saith the Lord" (Isa 58:1-14).

The fivefold purposes of fasting, as given to the Lord's people through the Prophet Isaiah in chapter 58: 6-7:

First, to loosen the **BANDS OF INIQUITY** and WICKEDNESS—the **Struggle** with sinful behaviors: anger, rage, theft, lying, strife, contention, discord, disputes, despair, envy, pride, hatred, fornication, jealousy, fleshly tendency, immodesty, idolatry

(Rom 7:14-20).

Secondly, to UNDO **HEAVY BURDENS**—the **Challenges** of Life: physical health, emotional health, behavioral health, disabilities, intellectual challenges, financial challenges, wayward children, broken-heartedness, trauma and tragedy, deaths, accidents, disasters, strained relationships, persecutions, and unforgiveness (Matt. 5: 1-12).

Thirdly: FREEDOM FOR **ENSLAVED and OPPRESSED**— usurped, forfeited; displaced agency: imprisoned, violent, terrorist, gang activity, unsafe neighborhoods, racism, racial disharmony, bigotry, children of oppressed, impoverished, poor, refugees, orphans, illiterate (Isaiah 60:1-2).

Fourth: to BREAK **YOKES and STRONGOLDS**—Casualties of Life: immorality, adultery, sexual perversion, same-sex attractions, addictions, drunkenness, promiscuity. Gangs, murder, valance, lasciviousness. Pornography, gambling, unbelief and doubt, filthy lucre, impatience, and love of money (Romans 8:13).

Fifth and Finally: RELIEF FOR **THE AFFLICTED**—Less Fortunate Outcast of Life: hungry, naked, homeless, needy, generational curse, care for relatives, household of God, orphans, motherless, widows, elderly, sick and the suffering, downtrodden (John 10: 10).

This young man believes the most effective of all the things a family member or any truly caring person can do is to continue praying and periodically mingle your prayers with fasting, making mention of the fact that whenever fasting is mentioned in scripture, it is usually followed by the mention of prayer. Therefore, proper fasting is most effective when combined with prayer. This prayer should be specific and focused. Every fast should begin with a prayer and a specific purpose in mind. The proper fast, as revealed in ancient times, included abstaining from food and drink for a specified period of time. It is apparent from the writings of Isaiah that the mode and purpose of fasting had become perverted by the Israelites. They had practiced fasting only as a method of humbling themselves and were going to great extents to appear unto men to fast. In the church, founded in 1830, which this young man has attended for nearly four decades, prior to 1844, the early members of the Church were instructed to hold...a fast day. That practice continues through to this day.

The biblical fast was from sundown to sundown, constituting a fast of twenty-four hours. If unable to fast for that full length of time, customarily, this young man would at least abstain from eating two consecutive meals, one day of the month. The value of the food not consumed by the young man in these two meals could/should be contributed as a fasting day donation for the benefit of the poor and needy. Therefore, according to Isaiah 58, fasting is a powerful type of spiritual worship and warfare intended to be done in secret unto God. However, obedience to *observing* a day of fasting is rewarded openly (see also Matt. 6: 16-18).

As a Christian believer and following the counsel of Church leaders, this young man has regularly observed this day of fast, more consistently in some periods of his life than in others. However, he testifies that the importance of fasting to his recovery was revealed to him one afternoon during a sacramental communion Church service. Such a profound impression it made on him that he remembers he left the service with a more positive resolve from that day forth to properly observe each day of fast. Specifically, he believes he *committed* to an unseen influence that day to fast at least one day each month and make fasting donations. To this date, as the young man is making this record, he has lived true to that **commitment**.

Initially, he was fasting in two or three separate twenty-four-hour periods in any given month. Progressively, as he **observed** frequent and consecutive periods of fasting, he began to notice he was gradually becoming more aware of the distinct reality of his spiritual and physical nature; his thoughts were becoming more spiritually mature. During this period, the young man received some vivid experiences confirming the effectiveness of purposeful fasting and praying.

A dramatic manifestation occurred during a time when their son was grappling with his own personal struggles, including undiagnosed depression, and our family was deep in denial about it such that he would typically become angry with us and disappear for weeks and months at a time after we attempted to confront him about some of his destructive behaviors. Having already developed a firm testimony in fasting and prayer over a period of several years, this young man decided to fast this particular day to hear from his son. This young man acknowledges a prompt miraculous response from God on their behalf; within twenty-four hours, their son called, and all was well with him.

During the following months, this young man resorted to fasting and praying on several other occasions to hear from their son. Every time, without fail, they would hear from him. Not always as quickly, but never more than two to three days. This young man bears his personal witness and solemn testimony of this truth to the family members of an addicted person. He knows fasting and praying is an effective and proven process to partition the Lord's help to intervene on behalf of your loved one to break the **denial syndrome**. Until this denial cycle is completed, the addicted person may receive help and assistance, but they will not accept it.

This brings this young man back to his central point again: reemphasizing the need for this to be understood by the caring loved ones and the addicted. Deal with the D.E.N.I.A.L. first! **(Romans 12: 1-2)**

16

THE FAST DAY

FASTING INVITATION LETTER

Greetings: Relatives, Church Family, Friends, Acquaintances, [All Readers];

This young man is sending you this correspondence because he feels assured his experiences warrant his impressions, his gratitude, and his desires be made known to each of you.

An unknown Christian philosopher has said, "Life must be lived forward"—a day, a week, a month, a year, a decade, a century at a time—"but Life is understood backward" as we take the time to remember, review, and reflect upon yesterdays and yesteryears. Accordingly, the desires, impressions, and gratitude this young man feels inclined to proclaim at this time are a result of reflecting, pondering, and reviewing lingering memories from across six decades of his life journey. The impressions from his life journey are laced with choice experiences that taught him inexplicably that life's battles and struggles are not against "flesh and blood." Personal life experiences suggest that the core battles for him during his life course have been, and continue to be, spiritual in essence. He argues that the most challenging experiences of his life course have been the offspring of his fleshly lusts and the influence of principalities, powers, rulers, and the pressures of wickedness and darkness (Eph 6:12; Titus 3:1).

Therefore, this young man believes the weapons of our warfare must become spiritual as well. My gratitude oozes from within my inner being as I try to humbly and calmly contemplate the goodness, awesomeness, and wisdom of the Almighty Most High God. Furthermore, it is my burning desire for each of us to come together, fit in the armor for spiritual warfare, and begin taking back stolen territory—breaking chains, strongholds, yokes, bondages, and releasing captives, triumphantly in the sacred name of our Almighty Most High God. What are spiritual weapons of war?

Spiritual weapons, by design, are meant to "loose bands of wickedness, undo heavy burdens, free the oppressed, break yokes, and break strongholds" (Isaiah 58: 6). Furthermore, there are corresponding blessings endowed upon those who properly and appropriately engage spiritual warfare using these weapons. These promised blessings do include but are not limited to health, inspiration, revelation, protection, divine guidance, provisions, and exposure to deceitful and evil darkness (Isaiah 58: 8-12). Nonetheless, the unintended blessings from the use of these spiritual weapons will "feed the hungry, clothe naked, shelter homeless, and care for our relatives," according to the Word of God (Isaiah 58: 7). What are these spiritual weapons of war? Are you prepared to arm yourself?

Effective execution and engagement in spiritual warfare demands a specific attitude, behavior, and observance (Matt: 6: 16-18). Acceptable and successful deployment of our spiritual weapons is contingent upon our disposition, attitude, motives, countenance, mercy, relationship with others, personal and private devotion, and our reverence towards Almighty God (Isaiah 58: 9-14). What are these spiritual weapons of war? Are you prepared to arm yourself?

FASTING

Suggested Observance

1. Begin after the dinner meal of your selected day. (Suggested between 6:00 - 8:00 p.m.)

2. After the meal, kneel in a formal prayer to begin the fast in which you will deny yourself for the next two meals, including breakfast and lunch, as a living sacrifice to the Lord for the purpose of petitioning, asking, seeking, and knocking on the door of the Lord for his divine intervention into our lives.

3. After the formal prayer, resolve to refrain from any food or drink during the specified period of the fast. However, if you are on medications or diagnosed and challenged with health issues, do what is in your best interest; all you can do is all you can do, judge for yourself.

4. There should be a concerted effort to deny food or drink for the next two meals on the upcoming day. Therefore, you will sacrifice your breakfast and lunch meals to the Lord.

5. Pray before going to sleep that night, a personal and specific prayer as an individual or an arranged group or family prayer, whereas you petition the Lord for a specific blessing to be received and manifested and consecrate your fasting efforts to that end, in accordance with the perfect will of the Lord.

6. Spend some time reading the Word of God before going to sleep; this can be very enlightening, inspiring, and even revelatory. This can be a very special and sacred time to be alone with the Spirit of the Lord.

7. Sacrifice breakfast and spend that time, even more time, if you can, reading the word of God before you get wrapped and wound up in your day; remember to say your prayers and remember your requests and supplications to the Lord.

8. Throughout the morning, be mindful of your specific personal prayer to the Lord. During your period of fasting, think of the person or persons whom you would like to improve your relationship with—family, friends, neighbors, or anyone else in your circles of acquaintances.

9. Sacrifice your lunch meal and spend some of the time reading in the word of God, praying in the spirit, praying in secret (out loud if possible), in your mind, or in your heart. Remember to be specific and ask for the perfect will of God to be done in our lives and in the lives of others.

10. Just before partaking of the dinner meal, and before your blessing on your food, have a formal prayer to end your fast and set apart the sacrificed meals and that time of sacrifice to the Lord, willfully giving Him full access into any areas of your life, particularly that area that is most important to your spiritual growth at this time. Bless your food and enjoy your meal in the name of Jesus Christ.

17

REFLECTION

THIS YOUNG MAN IS SAYING... from his own private and personal experiences, he feels the addict should be sternly confronted as soon as possible after suspicion of illegal drug use, chemical dependency, or drug abuse of destructive addictive behaviors, especially if the suspected drug user is a past drug abuser.

Furthermore, this young man advises loved ones to stand firm, avoid the D.E.N.I.A.L. syndrome trap, be genuinely concerned for the welfare of the user, and confront them under the auspices of *tougher love*. Upset the apple cart. This young man further advises the **loved ones of addicts to become educated about addiction, relapse, and the recovery process.** It will be difficult to continue *tougher love* for very long, remaining genuinely concerned for the addict still active in addiction, denying, refusing to stop using, and displaying addictive behaviors. It will be next to impossible if all family members are uneducated about chemical dependency, addiction, relapse, and the recovery process.

THIS YOUNG MAN IS SAYING... from his own personal experience, a family member becoming educated about chemical dependency, addiction, relapse, and the recovery process could be the difference between relapse recovery, homelessness, or death. Chemical dependency, addiction, relapse, and destructive addictive behaviors all follow a predictable cycle. Nevertheless, although addiction is treatable, active addicts live a life of jails, institutions, and graves without treatment. Therefore, continuing tough or tougher love for the addict is a tall order when caring family members are under the stress, the strain, and the uncertainty of active addiction. Besides, the recovery itself is uncertain; usually, less than 8% of those initially entering traditional 12-step rehab program institutions remain clean and sober (AA World). However, Christ-centered recovery programs with a focus on educating those challenged by chemical dependency, addiction, relapse, and other destructive addictive behaviors are experiencing greater than 50% success rates (Celebrate Recovery).

"Remember! You are a soul worth saving."

This is something the young man remembered his wife had said to him one day. Her statement touched him very tenderly, made tears swell up in his eyes, and caused him to cry. Underneath the destructive addictive behavior of your loved one is that not really bad of a person that everyone remembers and sees in their mind's eye.

"Remember! You, the addict, and your loved one, the addict, is a soul worth saving."

18

F.R.O.G.

The difficulty of recovery for the young man was for him to first come to the understanding that he was addicted; therefore, he was an addict, and **he needed to begin doing something different because something needed to change.** Then, the young man needed to be convinced to follow an evidence-based course and plan of action that has been proven successful in arresting, mortifying, and putting addiction to death. The longer the addicted, the non-addicted, and the co-dependents and enablers remain in D.E.N.I.A.L., the more devastating the effects on the total dynamics of the family. Eventually, addiction becomes more difficult to stop than stopping a fully loaded freight train with a full head of steam, sprinting out of control and on a downhill track.

One day, a few months after the death of Junior Frog, the young man was not having a good day. His car had broken down, and he had walked to the auto parts store. First, so that the reader may fully understand the impact of the coming exchange, let it be known that this young man had learned to mask his feelings from all others. The young man was living life in a self-imposed eternal state that W.E.B Dubois referred to as "double consciousness" in *The Souls of Black Folks* (Dubois, 1903).

The young man was trying to be strong for his family, but on this day, he was surely hurting inside. He previously indicated that he felt like someone had reached into his chest cavity and snatched out his heart and other vital organs. He felt as if he was wandering around in an inner excruciating pain. Literally, the young man was meandering around, waiting to topple over and die so someone could push him into a grave, cover him over, and put him out of his everlasting misery.

However, this day, he had walked a minimal distance to the auto parts store because he was working on the car; he had left the car parked at home. Feeling lower than low, the depressed young man was feeling worthless, deserted, humiliated, frustrated, really lonely, hopeless, helpless, abandoned, and confused. He paused briefly, just outside the door of the auto parts store, on the sidewalk in front of the store. On the way into the store, he passed a woman who spoke to him. She said your usual casually polite salutations: "Hello, how are you doing." To which his usual pretentious response would have been, "Hello, I am doing fine. How are you doing?" This day, however, in the spring of 2002, the young man told that lady the truth. He looked her straight in the eyes and said, "You know, I am not having a good day at all. In fact," he said, "this is one of the most difficult days of my life.

He continued by telling her that a few months ago, he had gone through the most devastating event of his entire life. The young man went through and shared a few quick, brief experiences related to the death, burial, and funeral services of my 26-year-old firstborn child. As he was speaking these words to the lady, tears swelled up in his eyes. The lady looked him straight in the eyes and then gave him a message that he believed was straight from the bosom of a loving, caring, eternal God who knew just the words he needed. She said to him, "Everything will be all right; you just have to... *'remember the frog.'*"

I said, "What did you say?"

She repeated herself: "Everything will be all right; you just have to... *'remember the frog.'*"

I said, "Ok, I will always remember the frog," I had agreed to it, but I did not know what she meant by it. She looked at me in my eyes and said for the third time, "Everything will be all right; you just have to... *'remember the frog.'*" Then, the kind lady spelled out the word frog. "F.R.O.G. Fully Rely on God, and everything will be alright." To this very day, I do not know who that woman was, where she went, and I never had a chance to say thank you, but she gave me a word from God that day, and I have never forgotten to *REMEMBER THE F.R.O.G.*

19

THE ART OF LIVING

Life Lessons, Trials, Tests, Obstacles, Failures, Challenges, Grief & Disappointments
The final outcome is never as bad,
as it seems it will be in the beginning.
There is an unseen hand ALWAYS at work.
Divine intervention is never late,
But always on time and rarely early.
All you can do is all you can do;
Then, and only then, it is all you can do.
"GREATNESS CAN ONLY BE ACHIEVED WHEN ALL THAT CAN BE DONE,
HAS BEEN DONE."

LIFE DECISIONS
Early in the journey through life
A person finds themselves at
A crossroad *and* must choose

One of two roads of great highways.
THE right:
leading to progress
and happiness
THE wrong:
leading to
retardation and sorrow.
There exists an eternal law.
That each human soul,
Through the choices they make,
Will shape their own destiny.
Our Success or Failure,
Peace, Happiness or Misery,
Depends on the choices
We make each day.

20/20 HINDSIGHT
Autumn dawns on my eternal summer;
Young is old, an internal bummer.
I no more than followed the sun.
"Retire from the grind" now,
But I chose the fun.
I shunned work responsibility;
Used my hands, making life frivolity;
I could have been someone,
Many opportunities, but I chased the sun.
Overcast; Winter coming; Cold;
Stop grind, before you're too old.

What If?
Imagine the year
2029, and 2039;
Where will U be?
What will U be doing?
How will What U do today influence
Ten or Twenty years from now?

GOOD IS THE ENEMY OF GREATNESS
Good Performance
It is not enough.
Going to the next level
Requires GREAT Performance.
GREATNESS CAN ONLY BE ACHIEVED WHEN ALL
THAT CAN BE DONE,
HAS BEEN DONE.

GIFT of STRUGGLE

A man saw a butterfly on the sidewalk, locked in **a seemingly hopeless struggle** to free itself from its now useless cocoon. Feeling pity and sorrow, the man carefully cut away the cocoon and set the butterfly free. To his dismay, it lay on the sidewalk, convulsed weakly for a while, and died. A biologist said: "That was the worst thing you could have done! **A butterfly needs to struggle** to develop muscles to fly. Robbing him of struggle, **you made him too weak to live.**"

KARMA

Cheaters Never
Prosper
In the Long Run,
And
In Real-Life,
U Reap What
U Sow.

KNOWLEDGE

He who Knows
and Knows he Knows
is Wise;
However, He who Knows
But Knows Not that
He Knows, Is yet still ignorant,
Unlearned, Not Matured,
and Foolish

IGNORANCE
He who Thinks
He Knows, But Knows not;
Is yet Ignorant,
Foolish, Immature, Unlearned;
And drives Away HIM
who is Wise,
And Quench Even the Holy Spirit.

WHO AM I?
One of a kind:
Rare, Unique and Valuable;
The Enemy Is the Inner ME;
Too Soon Old & Too Late Smart.

WHY AM I HERE?
The Main Thing;
Is to Keep the Main Thing,
The Main Thing.
Listen; Obey; Think;
Observe, Retain, and Reflect.

INTEGRITY—To Thy Own Self Be True

WHEN THE STUDENT IS READY
The Teacher Will Appear

ONE OF A KIND

There has never been another person
exactly like me, in the history of mankind,
nor will there ever be.
God, our Heavenly Father, has made me an original,
one-of-a-kind:
UNIQUE, RARE, and VALUABLE.
God said it; I believe it,
That settles it!

CAUSE & EFFECT

We are Agents to Ourselves;
We act by way of
Choices and Decisions;
We are acted upon by
Choices and decisions made by Others.
Our World is Governed by Cause and Effect.

NOT A THING

Nothing! Absolutely Nothing;
Not One Thing!
Ever happens in this World by Accident.

TWO SHALL BECOME ONE

Searching to understand the link of our physical world to
the spiritual world, I reflect
upon *marriage—the* sacred, holy union of male and female.
Let no man put asunder what

God put it together. Therefore, the actions of the one flesh cannot be separated from the

actions of the other.

The two shall **become** one.

I realize that whatever affects one flesh affects the other. The marriage covenant binds

two individuals together to become one flesh. Do not forget! You reap what you sow.

Therefore, seeds sown by one produce harvest for the other, regardless of the Sower.

The two shall **become** one.

Furthermore, be not unequally yoked to unbelievers. Believers can produce good

harvests; however, the unbelieving can produce a harvest in opposition to believers. One

spouse is a Sower, but they both shall reap what was sown.

The two shall **become** one.

My house and I will serve the living God.

2 SHALL BECOME 1

Perfect and Righteous are not the same.

Saying what is right with scripture

Is being a perfect man;

Able to control his whole body.

Righteousness is of Jesus Christ,

Not what we do or say.

The two shall **become** one.

Unconfused and Unrepeated;

Wickedness Brings Tribulations;

Trials, Tests, and Temptations—of the Devil. Righteous and Wicked Tormented

Low-down, Dirty, Snake—Lucifer

The devil—the Father of Lies.
The two shall **become** one.
Therefore,
One Spouse Sows the Other Reaps;
The Other Spouse Sows One Reaps
Two Flesh Joined as One;
Two Bringing Fruit, One Life.
The two shall **become** one.
Lean to the Spirit that entices you to pray;

THE TWO SHALL BECOME ONE

We are born separate and formed individually,
but we are to join together to **become** one.
The two shall **become** one.
2 shall **become** 1:
One Man + **One** Woman
Two Flesh shall become
One FLESH

2 BE 1

The two shall become one
1+1=2
½ (1+1) = (2) ½
(½ + ½) = (1)
1 = 1
Two Flesh
Shall Become One
2 B 1
Multiply Your Better Half

BECOME BORN AGAIN

1 M.A.N. + 1 W.O.M.A.N. + G O D = A DIVINE SPECIES

Greater is He that is within thee,

Than he that is in the world.

20

INTRO TO AA—ADDICTION DENIAL

"Hello, I lift my voice from the dust
   to introduce myself to all of you,
   maybe even to myself.
   Maybe *once* is all it takes…
   My name is AA—Addiction Denial.
   A Chemical-dependency disease,
   Nicknamed: Addict, Junky, Wine-O, Alcoholic,
   Pothead, Crack-Head, Chicken-Head,
   Drunk, Geek Monster…
   My Relatives' names are:
   Social Drinker, Casual Smoker,
   Recreational User, Week-ender
   Party Animal, Pill Popper…
   My power is:
   I make a good first impression.
   I make you feel good.
   I make you believe we belong together.
   I will ease your pain and relieve the pressure.

I can even cover up problems...
The thing I do best is D.E.N.I.A.L. and
You <u>D</u>on't <u>E</u>ven <u>N</u>o! It's <u>A</u> <u>L</u>ie.
I am Cunning, Baffling, and Powerful....
I am Persistent, Relentless, and Manipulative.
I know more about you than you know about me.
This helps me to form a long-lasting relationship...
I will energize you.
I will accept you just as you are.
I know your failures, where your hurt is from.
I destroy your secrets and dreams.
I use a stronghold for a lasting relationship...
My presence comes as flashes of insight,
Marked by statements from you, such as:
WHY DID I DO THAT?
I MUST BE CRAZY!
I AM JUST SO STUPID!
I AM LOSING MY MIND!
YOU CAN'T BELIEVE I DID THAT!
Our relationship is a promise to be long-term,
When you say the all-convincing:
"I will never do that again."
This is the sure sound of my presence...
I can convince you to Beg, Borrow, and Steal
Confess and deny my presence.
I am, whoever you say I am,
Spoken from your mouth
Gives me permission to stay and abide
Friends and companion
Riding together forever.

21

SUMMARY OF F.R.O.G. PRINCIPLES

Principle: **FROG IN THE MILK**

Keep on keeping on, and do not give up. Look around, help is not far away.

Principle: **THE COOKED FROG SYNDROME**

Beware of it, avoid it, and get out of it: "The Comfort Zone Trap."

Stop thinking all is well, or you may end up a cooked frog.

Principle: **THE F.R.O.G.S. DILEMMA**

Stop your train wreck now;

Get rid of your frog Dilemmas today,

Do not put it off one more day.

There is no need to procrastinate; now is the time.

Principle: **FIVE FROGS ON A LOG**

Go ahead and decide to jump. The recovery pond is one decision away.

Just do it now; go ahead and get wet.

Principle: **REMEMBER THE F.R.O.G.**

F.R.O.G. - Fully Rely On God

22

PONDERIZATION OF LIFE
F.R.O.G.S.

Life, even with all of its twists and turns, continues to unfold, undoubtedly just as planned by the Creator of heaven and earth. Recognizing that all of life's experiences have made this young man what he is today. If any facet of his life were left out or changed, he would not be totally who he has become today. This young man is an exquisite and unique, wonderfully made child of the Most High God. He was put here on this earth with a created purpose, a purpose to become that included being endowed with an intense love and adoration of the life journey.

Inarguably, undoubtedly, and with absolute certainty, this young man reminds himself today, first and foremost, that he is a child of the Most High God and was created by the Supreme Creator of Heaven, Earth, and all that exists. There is an exclusive divine purpose for which he was created to fulfill. The Adversary—the Father of Lies, the Accuser, the Author of Confusion, that low-down dirty snake Lucifer—the devil, like a roaring lion, goes about seeking whosoever he may detract from their created purpose; his ultimate desire is only to steal our joy and peace, kill our hope, destroy our ambitions, and devour our potential.

It is this young man's prayer of gratitude that he is no longer counted amongst the captives of the adversary as a causality of the raging battle of spiritual warfare. For this purpose, this young man desires guidance, further tutoring, and spiritual insight in this most serious matter presently before him: his divinely created life purpose. As the young man contemplates and ponders his adversarial life trials and challenges in the art of living, nonetheless, he is filled with the desire to become that unto which he was created to become firmly committed in the face of all opposition to continue to move forward in his quest as a human becoming.

Moreover, it is this young man's belief that surely, the spirits of Goodness and Mercy shall continue to follow him throughout all the remaining days of his life. His prayer is that the favor of God, through these spirits, shall overtake him, hedge up the way around him, and that he may not offend his Creator and Eternal Father. How grateful he is for the blessing of life and knowledge of the Lord as his personal Savior, even Jesus Christ. He humbly and with utmost sincerity asks forgiveness for his poor judgments, mistakes, sins, and shortcomings and prays that the consequences of his actions are not a hindrance unto those around him. Furthermore, it is this young man's prayer that he continues not to be blinded by the cunning deceit and whiles of the adversarial foes from the enemy.

I admit some of this young man's emotions and behaviors are especially difficult for him to fully master and control, particularly emotions and behaviors that are deeply rooted in unjust incidents and circumstances of the distant past. Be that as it may, from his experiences through chemical dependency, addiction, relapse, and destructive addictive behaviors, it has become his belief that the way to be released from the grips of influences from the past on his future emotions and behavior, he must first acknowledge the existence of these influences. Secondly, this young man must admit personal *"powerlessness and the unmanageability"* of the effects of such influences, being ever reminded this world is controlled by eternal governing laws of cause and effect.

Thirdly, this young man must admit and accept nothing is fortunate or unfortunate in the world as we travel the highways of this life course, realizing that it is an individual perspective that gives meaning to the happenings in our lives. Furthermore, it is his belief that God, our Creator, is in control of all things. Therefore, this young man also believes all things work together for a *perceived* good for those who love God and are created and called according to His purposes.

Keeping that in mind, finally, I must admit the present trials, adversity, and emotional struggles of his current situations are related to choices from his immediate and distant past. Additionally, he understands that there is, in fact, no right way to do a *wrong* thing. Consequently, this young man's desire is to do that which is right and most effective in his efforts to be released from the grips of the influences of the past. Moreover, his desire is to be an instrument of good in the hands of the Lord forever and always. Currently, the consequences of poor choices and errors in judgment are actively influencing the life choices before him on the pathway of his life journey.

Furthermore, in pondering the construct of his present reality, this young man seeks wisdom from the Spirit of the Lord, as a quiet, still, small whispering voice from heavenly realms, to enlighten his mind and reveal the perfect will of the Lord for this most challenging time in this young man's journey of life. Therefore, Lord, I am asking forgiveness for all impure thoughts, emotions, and actions, and I seek the companionship of the Holy Ghost to renew a right Spirit unto me in the name of Jesus Christ.

D.E.N.I.A.L

D.E.N.I.A.L.
D.E.N.I.A.L.
D.E.N.I.A.L.

The deadliest symptom of chemical-dependency addiction:
Ignoring Destructive Addictive Behavior
until it progresses "OUT OF CONTROL."
D.E.N.I.A.L. speaks statements like:
"You do not do this in our family!"
"You can stop it anytime you want to!"
"You are so stupid for doing that!"
"You will never do that again!"
"I cannot believe you did that!"
"You must be crazy!"
The TRUEST display of D.E.N.I.A.L. is:
YOU
Don't Even No! It's A Lie

YOU AND DENIAL

You and Denial
    YOU and D.E.N.I.A.L.
    Remember!
    When you hear yourself say?
    "I WILL NEVER DO THAT AGAIN."
    "I CAN STOP, ANYTIME I WANT TO."

U R N D.E.N.I.A.L.
    AND
    U
    Don't **E**ven **N**O! **I**T'S **A** **L**IE

25

REMEMBER, REMEMBER, REMEMBER

Remember, Remember, Remember

The tailor-made life experiences of this young man's more than six decades have helped him identify, adopt, and add to his repertoire of core life principles and beliefs. Among these beliefs is his acceptance and understanding that there are not any two days that are exactly alike. Therefore, no one really knows precisely what the next day in life or in the classroom of the school of Hard Knocks will bring. However, with absolute certainty, now as a certified "Knucklehead" and an honors graduate of that university of knowledge, this young man knows as long as he remembers the frog, as his guardian angelic messenger had instructed him many years earlier, everything will be alright.

As Knucklehead Young Man soothes his mind with the previous sobering but somber thought, he begins to perceive a powerful presence coming into his inner conscious awareness. Gathering his composure, Knucklehead Young Man becomes mindful of a feeling of profound relaxation, calmness, serenity, and peace coming over him. It was as if a solemn state of peacefulness was permeating into his present physical space, seemingly a type of osmosis and generating a profound, deeply felt, and invigorating feel-good sensation. Knucklehead Young Man further acknowledges that the more prevalent the powerful presence seems to come into his conscious awareness, the more he becomes filled with a state of hopeful expectancy and anticipation.

The feelings and sensations were similar to an experience etched in the memory of Knucklehead Young Man from an experience he had nearly twelve years earlier. However, he felt as if he was experiencing it all over again, as if it was happening now. The revelatory, illuminating, and enlightening experience from his past, when Knucklehead Young Man was being tormented by his frogs of life dilemma and had opened unto him early one morning as he was sitting in the back of his van, parked in a public city park. Previously, during this time in his life, Knucklehead Young Man had been classed as a #1knucklehead. However, advancing through the art of living, he developed a belief that maintaining a mindfulness of present-day moments and reflection on incidents of past days, weeks, years, decades, and centuries will reveal important life messages. Sometimes they can be significant messages relating to our divinely created purpose and passed along through persons who have crossed the path of our life course.

Mentally riding upon the rollercoaster of that very thought, Knucklehead Young Man began to sense, within his memory pathways, a recall of deceased relatives, friends, and other persons who had served as guardians of light across his life span. The first presence was the familiar messenger in the form of an inaudible voice message from his grandmother, relaying to the young man: "Do not be afraid, be of good courage, laugh, be happy, and continue to pursue your divinely created life purpose."

Suddenly, overshadowing the presence and inaudible voice of the familiar messenger was the presence of Knucklehead Young Man's grandfathers, Richard and Horace Campbell; his Aunts Jessie Mae and Great Aunt Beulah; two dear friends, George "Budd" Peterson and Vernon James Mays; his two sisters, Jacquelyn and Mamie; classmates Marshall and Karl; and his son Junior Frog.

Never before had Knucklehead Young Man been so overwhelmed with the magnitude of such profound presence from beyond the realms of the eternities. As he began to contemplate the significance of this unique experience, he was carried away in the confined annals of memories of past events, incidents, and experiences stored within the treasury of his mind. Simultaneously, it was transcribed and telegraphed into his conscious awareness and made visible on the screen of his mind, not in words and letters, in such a manner as to be perfectly understood, but impossible to misunderstand the message.

The ongoing thoughts relating to Knucklehead Young Man's core beliefs, recently identified, adopted, and added to his repertoire of core life principles, were promptly resumed. However, the perceived message on the screen of his mind was to succinctly further skillful godly wisdom and understanding of Knucklehead Young Man's core life principles of belief. In preparation for his receiving further knowledge, wisdom, and understanding of eternal truths and the art of living, he needed for him to accept, understand, internalize, and commit to applying the principles to his daily life. He so agreed and was immediately submerged into a renewed and transformed perception of the life journey.

Knucklehead Young Man emerged from that state of consciousness with sure and undaunting confidence that life has an uncanny ability to navigate us through frogs of life and other tailor-made life experiences. Persistent, determined commitment to the art of living allows these experiences to be permitted into our circles of existence because they are designed to teach valuable life lessons that are intended to be passed on to others.

Keeping that thought in mind, Knucklehead Young Man remembers it was June 2013, twelve years following the death of Junior Frog; on a Saturday morning, Knucklehead Young Man had just left home driving to meet with some acquaintances. He was probably no more than three miles away from home. Surprisingly, what seemed to come out from nowhere there appeared a black Suburban, Expedition, and a Lincoln Navigator directly behind him; he could see in his rearview mirror. Just as the knucklehead young man noticed the vehicles riding close behind him, blue lights began to flash.

Immediately, without any prompting, the knucklehead young man began to perceive deep within his inner being a message from the powerful presence of the previously experienced past lives of family members and friends coming into his present moment of mindfulness. The message he received, although inaudible, unwritten, and perceived, in its essence, said: "Remember the frog, stop and fill your pockets; tomorrow you will be happy and sad." Knucklehead Young man also perceived an abiding assurance he was to: "Do not be afraid; be of good courage; be happy and laugh; and continue to pursue his life purpose."

The fading perception from deep within his inner being relayed to Knucklehead Young Man the essence of his newfound eternal truth: through the art of living, "life has the uncanny ability to navigate us through tailor-made life experiences" with GOD—THE Creator and Master Designer of events and incidents designed to teach valuable life lesson.

Therefore, Knucklehead Young Man knew he was entering a graduate school of life lessons in a classroom of the School of Hard Knocks. (It was as if time had stopped or only a few moments had passed since he left home before the blue lights flashed, and Knucklehead Young Man began receiving his inner perceptions and impressions).

As Knucklehead Young Man returned from his inner thoughts and impressions to be back in the present moment and the looming construct of his current reality, the unavoidable realism was blaring him in the face.

The vehicles were unmarked law enforcement automobiles, and they were pulling him over. As the officer came to the side of his car, Knucklehead Young Man was informed, "We have a murder warrant for the arrest of your son..."

Remember
  The F.r.o.g.
  Fully
  Rely
  On
  God

F.R.O.G.S. of LIFE
  Frustrations
  Rejections
  Opposition
  Grievances
  Sinful acts
  Five Frogs
  Sitting On a Log
  Decide, Ready to Get,
  But Nothing Changed Yet;
  Nothing Changes till Some Thing Changes;
  Only One Way Out,
  F.R.O.G.
  U Got to Get Wet

26

LIFE AND MEMORY

This chapter is dedicated to: The Life and Mempory of Twenty-six-year-old Darrel James Campbell, Jr. 1975-2001.

This young man, finding himself ignorant of the associated symptoms, distinct challenges, and the difficulty of treating substance abuse, chemical dependency, and depression, and being unable to help his own struggling son, he turns to heaven from whence came his help. This young man has been persuaded and enticed by Old Testament writings recorded by Hosea the Prophet, wherein the prophet declares, instructs, and then explains, in chapter 4:6, that Christian believers—Children of GOD—THE Creator and Master Designer— are being destroyed by life circumstances (frogs) because of a "lack of knowledge" or the rejection of skillful godly wisdom. Furthermore, failure to increase in understanding and in the application of wisdom from GOD—THE Creator and Master Designer; and rejection of other evidence-based sources of knowledge and insight from secular, scientific, academic, School of Hard Knocks, and other personal life experiences hinders Christians' efforts to put to death the frogs in their life.

Consequently, as a result, primarily motivated by the death of his son on November 4, 2001, this young man began a quest seeking, pursuing, sorting, and acquiring increased knowledge, wisdom, understanding, and insight into the symptoms of depression, denial, substance abuse, chemical dependency, relapse, and destructive addictive behaviors.

However, this young man's journey of self-motivated discovery was directed by a concerted, dogmatic, persistent, unwavering focus on the most successful and most effective evidenced-based secular, academic, scientific, and spiritual principles relative to recovering from the frogs of life. Furthermore, and in consequence of this young man's twenty-year pursuit, the following bibliography represents a thumbnail listing of his perusal of secular, academic, religious, and spiritually inspired writings; insights, principles, teachings, beliefs, and testimonies from others as well as his own personal testimonials relating to death to the frogs of life.

Moreover, this young man dedicates his pursuit to obtaining knowledge and this partial listing on behalf of his deceased firstborn son, Darrell "Junior Frog" Campbell. This collective list of materials was carefully gleaned by this young man and explored during a journey of increasing his understanding of destructive addictive behaviors and death to frogs of life.

This listing is highlighted to emphasize the intensity of commitment and devotion required to change the paradigms of belief relating to hi-jacked brain disorders—chemical-dependency destructive addictive behaviors and to facilitate permanent change, peace, serenity, recovery, and death to frogs of life.

BIBLIOGRAPHY

Ackerman, Diane. *Why the Leaves Turn Color in the Fall.* Random House, Inc. New

York, New York. 1990. n. page. Print

Alcoholics Anonymous: Third Edition. Alcoholics Anonymous World Services, Inc.

New York City, New York, 1976

Allen, James. As A Man Thinketh. Devorss & Company. Marina del Rey, CA

Baby 2 See Fetal Development Information. Web March 21, 2012

Baby Center: Surprising Facts About Births. Web March 22, 2012

Cause and Effect. Understanding the Essenic Theorem. The Principles of Karma

www.thenazareneway.com/cause Web May 17, 2012

Child Study Center (CSC) in New York City was founded in 1997 at Bellevue Hospital

Center, with Harold S. Koplewicz, M.D., as Director. 8 March 2012

Compton's Encyc. 1999 Addiction & Withdrawal

Conference Report, Oct. 1986, 20; *Ensign*, Nov. 1986, 17; Conference Report, Oct.

1989, 16; *Ensign*, Nov 1989, 14). The Church of Jesus Christ of Latter-Day

Cowen, Tyler. *The Great Stagnation.* Dutton Penguin Group, Inc. New York, New

York. February 2011. 162-165 Print.

Darwin, Charles Robert. *On Origin of Species.* Oxford University Press, USA

1/1/2009. n. page. Print

Ferrante, Joan. *Seeing Sociology: An Introduction.* Wadsworth Cengage Learning,

Canada 2011. Print

Flanagan, Geraldine L. *Beginning Life: The Marvelous Journey from Conception to Birth.* DK Publishing Inc., New York, New York 1996. 147 Print

Hamlin, H. *Life or Death by EEG: Journal of the American Medical Association.* 12

October, 1964. 198-201 Print.

Holy Bible, King James Version: New Testament with Explanatory Notes and Cross

References To the Standard Works of The Church of Jesus Christ of Latter-Day

Holy Bible, New International Version: The NIV Worship Bible Containing the Old

Testament and The New Testament. Zondervan, Grand Rapids, Michigan 1984

Kane, Thomas R., Acting Director, Bureau of Prisons Office of General Counsel,

Federal Bureau of Prisons, 320 First St., NW., Washington, DC 20534.Under §

505.2, the Director of the Bureau of Prisons determined that, based on fiscal

the year 2010 data, the fee to cover the average annual cost to confine an inmate in

a Community Corrections Center for Fiscal Year 2010 was $25,838.

Kendall, Diana Elizabeth, Social Problems in a Diverse Society

(5 Edition) Boston: Allyn and Bacon Feb 2009 (p. 162)

LDS Family Services. Addiction Recovery Program: A Guide to Addiction Recovery

and Healing. The Church of Jesus Christ of Latter-day Saints. Salt Lake City,

Utah 2005

Lemonick, Michael D. and Alice Park, "The Science of Addiction," Time, July 16

2007, 44.

Life Cycle, Human –Biology Encyclopedia – cell, body, process, system,

different, DNA, organs, blood, hormone,

major. www.biologyreference.com /Life-Cycle. Web Mar 2012

Lynskey, Michael T., Ph.D., et al., "Escalation of Drug Use in Early-Onset Cannabis

Users v Co--twin Controls," Journal of the American Medical Association, Vol.

289 No. 4, January 22/29, 2003, p. 432

Mandino, Og. The Return of The Ragpicker, Bantam Books Doubleday Dell

Publishing Group, Inc, New York, New York, February 1993, 136

Moore, Keith L. *The Developing Human.* 3rd ed. Philadelphia, PA: W.

B. Saunders, Co.1982. 314 Print.

Narcotics Anonymous: Fifth Edition. Narcotics Anonymous World Service Office, Inc.

Van Nuys, CA 1988

National Center for Addiction and Substance Abuse (NCASA). Columbia University

National Institute on Drug Abuse (NIDA) Pub Number: 09-4180

Published: October 1999 **Revised:** April 2009

National Institutes of Health. Drugs, Brains, and Behavior: The Science of Addiction.

Publication 10-5605 National Institute on Drug Abuse (NIDA) August 2010.

Neurological Health Charities of Canada (NHCC) My Brain Matters

http://www.mybrainmatters.ca/news/07-15-2010/brains-matter-

putting-most-vital-and-least-understood-organ-ahead-pack Website

30 November 2012

Pareto's Principle: The 80-20 Rule by Arthur W. Hafner, Ph.D. March 31,

http://www.bsu.edu/libraries/ahafner/awh-th-math- pareto.html Website 28 November 2012

Peck, M. Scott, M.D. The Road Less Traveled. Simon & Schuster 25th Anniversary

Edition-Touchstones Books. Safety Harbor, FL 1/07/2003

Phelps, Janice, MD. and Alan Edward, The Hidden Addiction, 1986

Saladin, Kenneth S. *"Anatomy and Physiology."* 2nd ed. New York:

McGraw-Hill, 2001. 145 Print

Substance Abuse and Mental Health Services Administration

(SAMHSA). *Results from the 2006 National Survey on Drug Use*

and Health: National Findings (Office of Applied Studies,

NSDUH Series H-32, DHHS Publication No. SMA 07-4293).

Rockville, MD, 2007

Tracy, Brian. The Psychology of Achievement: Six Keys to Personal Power. Institute

for Executive Development. Nightingale-Conant Corporation. Chicago, Illinois

1984, Audiocassette Program

University Of California, Los Angeles (2000, November 10). Nicotine Causes

Selective Degeneration in Brain, UCLA Neuroscientists Report. *ScienceDaily.*

Retrieved April 6, 2012, from
http://www.sciencedaily.com/releases/2000/11/001110073314.htm
Waitley, Denis E. The Psychology of Winning: Ten Qualities of a Total Winner. The
Human Resources Company. Nightingale-Conant Corporation. Chicago, Illinois
1978. Audiocassette Program
www.health.harvard.edu/mentalextra; www.health.harvard.edu; How addiction hijacks the brain Harvard Health Publishing Harvard Medical School; Harvard Mental Health Letter Published: July 2011
Website 22 March 2019
www.ronpaul2012.com; http://www.issues2000.org/tx/Ron_Paul_Drugs.htm
Website 28 November 2012
(SAMHSA) Substance Abuse and Mental Health Services
Administration. *Results from the 2006 National Survey on Drug Use and Health: National Findings* (Office of Applied Studies,
NSDUH Series H-32, DHHS Publication No. SMA 07-4293).
Rockville, MD, 2007